Python - Learn a New Skill Today

Lab 2: Business Expenses

Cathy Young

Table of Contents

4. Categorize Data

5. Output to Excel

6. Python Basics

7. Conclusion

1. Getting Started

In this chapter, we discuss

The Lab
Python
What's Next?

Are you curious about the Python language and wondering how to read and write Excel files efficiently? This book uses the format of a hands-on lab to create a complete program, with simple code examples that gather and categorize business expense details.

The lab uses the "openpyxl" functions to read, write, and format Excel objects. We'll also use dictionaries and lists with the data to drastically improve performance. The code is organized around several lab functions. The compartmentalized functions provide a logical stopping place if you want to take a break, and make it easier to "test" parts of your code and know they're working OK.

The step-by-step examples walk through each line of code with numbered examples, diagrams and tables. The written explanation and graphics highlight the line numbers in the code, so you can follow along and visualize the code running. If you'd like more information on a particular concept, there are links to the Python Basics chapter with extensive details and examples.

The book content follows an organized outline structure, in case you want to zero in on a particular task, such as "Add Expenses to the Sum Totals." This structure is mirrored in the Table of Contents to simplify locating a particular topic. I've also provided an extensive Index as a reference.

The lab also imports optional components that are commonly included in Python distributions like Anaconda. We'll extend Python's standard library with functions from the "openpyxl," "os," "sys", "string," and "datetime" libraries. To learn more about libraries, check out libraries for web scraping, json, charting, images, statistics, and more at https://pypi.org.

1.1 The Lab

This lab has several Python script files. A script is a simple text file with the ".py" extension. After setting up your Python environment in Chapter 2, the lab itself has three parts. Part 1 is the preliminary work of gathering data, and includes the main body of the program. Throughout the code we'll branch off and call "functions" and use other libraries. Part 2 categorizes the business expenses and computes sum totals. Finally, Part 3 outputs and formats the Excel file.

1.2 Anaconda & Spyder

Download the free Anaconda Distribution that includes Python version 3.x. When prompted, update your Path settings. The install takes a while, so you might want to grab a cup of coffee or something. For this lab I am using a Mac, and I'll point out the "os" module methods that vary slightly from a Mac to Windows computer.

Spyder is an Integrated Desktop Environment or IDE. Spyder includes an Editor, Console or Spyder Shell, Variable Explorer, a Help module, and other tools. These modules are displayed in "Panes" in Spyder.

On a Windows machine, launch Spyder from the Start Menu in the Anaconda folder. On a MAC computer, open the Anaconda Navigator and launch "Spyder."

A Spyder layout with three panes is shown in the next diagram. You can return to the default layout at any time from the View menu under Windows - Layouts. You can close or open other panes to suit your preferences. Launch Spyder from the Start Menu, in the Anaconda folder.

1.   The **Editor** pane is where you type your code and create your script files.

2.   The **Variable Explorer** pane lists variables in the current program scope after you run the code.

3.   The iPython **Console** or Python shell is located in the lower right panel by default. When you start Spyder, the Console prompt is **In[1]:**.

4.   When you click "Run," ▶ the results are output to the Console. When you type a command in the Console, Python immediately runs the command. The Console is useful when debugging or experimenting with different statements for your code.

5. Results displayed in the Console include code output and error messages. For example, if you use the print() method, the results are output to the Console window. In the example below, the **Console** displays "**Welcome to Project1.1.py**."

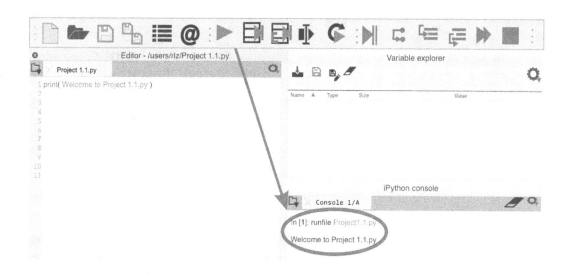

Figure 1.1   The iPython Console

Run a Python Script

With Spyder open, click on the File menu, and then click on "Open." Browse to the directory with your script files to open your *<script.py>* file. To run the code, click on the green arrow or use the Run menu, as shown below.

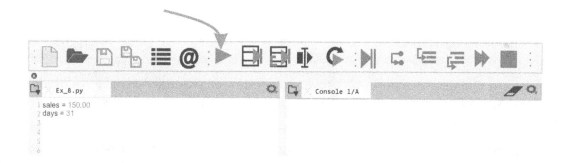

Figure 1.2   Run a Script File

Initially, the Console window displays **In [1]:**. After I click "**Run**," the Console window changes, as shown below. The first output line displays the name of the program file and the working directory.

In [1]:   runfile('...lab2.py', wdir= '.../lab2')

Stop a Program or Restart the Kernel

Click within the Console window and *press any key* followed by "Cntrl C" to stop program execution with a keyboard interrupt. You can also select "Restart kernel" from the "**Consoles**" menu.

Adding a "**break**" statement to your code causes program execution within that code block to stop. For example, if you are inside a loop, the "break" statement halts the loop, exits the loop, and continues running the next code block.

Help

In Spyder, click on the View menu and click "Panes" to open the "Help" pane. The Help pane can display details about functions and methods. In the next example, information for the object "datetime.date" is displayed in the Help pane. This datetime. date() method takes 3 arguments: year, month, day.

Figure 1.3   Help for datetime.date Function

There is also an Online Help pane to browse an index of standard library modules, third party packages, and your own code. On the View menu, select Panes, and then scroll down to "Online Help."

Click on the Help menu and click on "Spyder Tutorial." The tutorial opens in the Help pane. The topic "Recommended first steps for Python beginners" is an excellent resource for new programmers.

The "Debugging" topic demonstrates how to look at your code while it's running, in effect, "debugging." While debugging, the Editor pane highlights the current line. This line is executed when you click "run current line" on the debug toolbar. Variable Explorer displays the values in each variable in the current context.

While I'm not going to go into a lot of detail on debugging and help topics, I did want to cover a few introspection functions.

Introspection

Introspection is the ability to determine information about live objects such as modules, classes, methods, and functions. You can easily tell the type of the object at runtime. Several functions help with introspection, as well as the "**inspect**" library.

*objectname***?**

dir()

help()

id()

repr()

type()

locals()

globals()

To inspect objects, execute statements in the **Editor** and **Console**, including statements with "Instrospection" functions that provide details about objects. The syntax varies depending on whether you are typing in the **Editor** or **Console** pane. The syntax is also specific to the type of object. In the case of data structures like lists, tuples, or dictionaries, you may want to see values for the entire list or the value of only a particular list item.

Using ? in the Console

For details on any object, in the **Console** type the object name followed by a question mark. There is no space between the object name and the question mark. For details on the object "**myfunction**," in the **Console** type the function name followed by a question mark, as shown below. The output includes the Signature, DocString, and the type of object.

In [**2**]: myfunction**?**

```
Signature: myfunction(str)
Docstring: <no docstring>
File:      ~//Ch 3 code/Functions/<ipython-input-8-df3069fd62ae>
Type:      function
```

This next example returns help for the max() function. You may want to compare this output to the __doc__ attribute in the "docstring" topic that follows.

```
In [5]: max?

Docstring:
max(iterable, *[, default=obj, key=func]) -> value
max(arg1, arg2, *args, *[, key=func]) -> value

With a single iterable argument, returns its biggest item. The default
keyword-only argument specifies an object to return if the provided
iterable is empty. With two or more arguments, return the largest
argument.

Type:      builtin_function_or_method
```

dir()

The function **dir()** displays all objects in the current local namespace, as shown in the next figure. After running the sample "*Project1.1.py*" script, the local scope changes. This script uses the "openpyxl" library to create the **ws4** object. For example, after running the "*Project1.1.py*" script, the dir() function displays relevant information about the program objects in the **Console**. Type the dir() command in the **Console** window.

```
iPython console

Console 1/A

`bfrmaxrow`,
`dif`,
`diffile`,
`exit`,
`get_ipython`,
`itemretired`,
`load_workbook`,
`quit`,
`rnfile`,
`wb1`,
`wb2`,
`wb4`,
`ws1`,
`ws2`,
`ws4`]

In [4]:
```

Figure 1.4   Objects in Current Local Scope

dir(object)

While the **dir()** function looks at all objects, the statement **dir(ws4)** takes the argument "ws4" and retrieves information on that particular object. In the **Console** window attributes specific to the **ws4** object are displayed, as shown below. The dir(*<object>*) function displays different attributes depending on the type of object you use for the argument.

There is quite a long list of valid attributes for the **ws4** object, and the next example only shows a few of the attributes. In particular, I'm interested in what functions I can use with the **ws4** object, and I've highlighted the "**delete_cols**" method.

Note, if you're using an older version of **openpyxl**, "**delete_rows**" might not be available. The **dir()** function is an easy way to check if a particular function or method should work with your code.

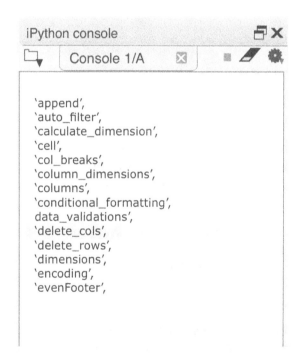

Figure 1.5   Valid Attributes for the ws4 Object

help()

The help() function invokes the help system for help with a module, function, class, method, keyword, or documentation topic. For example, when I type help(load_workbook) in the Console window, Python displays information specific to that method.

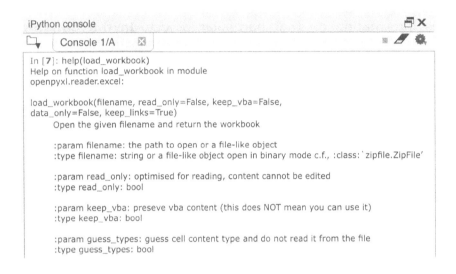

Figure 1.6   Help for load_workbook Method

Debug Mode

Use the **Debug** menu commands to step through the lines of code, or press Cntrl + F12 on a Windows computer to move to the next breakpoint. The Variable Explorer displays object values, changing over time as you step through the program code and the local scope changes.

In the **Editor**, double click on a line of code to set a breakpoint or press F12 on a Windows computer. When running a program in Debug Mode, a breakpoint pauses the program at that point, so that you can inspect the variable and object values in Variable Explorer or the Console. In the Editor, a red dot appears to the left of the line number with the breakpoint.

On the **Debug** menu, select 'debug' to launch the iPython debugger, or press Cntrl + F5 on a Windows computer. The prompt in the **Console** changes to ipdb>, indicating the iPython debugger is active.

If a program halts and displays a Traceback error, you can type **%debug** to start "Debug Mode,"

In the next example, there is a breakpoint • on line 3. The figure shows the **Editor** pane, as well as the **Console** pane, after I pressed Cntrl + F5 on a Windows computer to start debugging. Notice the **Console** prompt changed to **ipdb>**.

```
1 mystring = 'purple peanuts'
2
●3 print(mystring)
```

```
In [1]: debugfile('C:/SampleScript.py', wdir='C:')
>C:\SampleScript.py(1)<module>()
---->1 mystring = "purple peanuts"
      2 print (mystring)
```

ipdb>

In the **Console** pane, an arrow indicates the current line number, in this case, line 1. If Variable Explorer is not already open, on the **View** menu select "Panes," and then click on Variable Explorer. As I "**step-through**" the code, I want to watch the "mystring" object in Variable Explorer. At this point, Variable Explorer is empty because we have yet to run the first line of code to create the program's "namespace" in memory.

As you step through the code, the Editor highlights the current line.

Click the icon ⬛ to **Run the current line of code** or press **Cntrl + F10** on a Windows computer. The Python interpreter creates the object "mystring" and assigns the value "purple peanuts." This example of dynamic typing is one of the reasons I love Python. With one line of code, Python figures out the type of object to create and assigns a value.

End Debug Mode

To exit the debugger, type **q** or **quit** at the **Console** prompt and press enter, as shown below. If you are in an iPython Session in the **Console**, you may have to press **Esc + Enter**. You can also restart the kernel when you select "Restart Kernel" from the **Consoles** menu.

```
ipdb>C:\SampleScript.py(1)<module>()
      1 mystring = "purple peanuts"
      2
```

---->3 print (mystring)

ipdb>
ipdb>quit

In [**2**]:

Variable Explorer

As variables are created in your main program they are added to the "global scope" or namespace.The global scope is the first memory "stack." Variable Explorer displays objects in the current "scope" and is empty until you run the code to create the program's memory "namespace."

At this point in our example, **Variable Explorer** displays a row with the type of the "mystring" object, and the value I assigned in line 1.

Figure 1.7   The Variable Explorer Pane

Variable Explorer shows variables and objects in memory. If you don't see your object displayed in Variable Explorer, you need to execute that part of the program. If you're unsure if the variables are in scope, you could use the **locals()** function in the Console to see local variables.

To start fresh and clear program memory, in the Console use the magic function %Reset.

1.3 What's Next?

Your Lab environment is now setup. Let's move on to Chapter 2, where we look at the lab at a high level.

2. Lab Overview

In this Chapter, we discuss

Introduction

Categories

The Program Pseudocode

Before setting up your Python environment, let's briefly talk about the Excel files, Python modules, and the Lab 2 output. In later chapters we'll look at blocks of code and focus on one particular concept at a time.

- Structure of Lab 2 Excel Files

- A brief explanation of inputs and outputs of the Lab 2.py script

- An abbreviated list of the sixteen "steps" in the script.

As a reference, in the "Python Basics" chapter, I'll provide a brief description of the following Python objects and syntax.

- Python Syntax

- Structure of Excel Files

- Variables and Data Types

- Objects

- Statements

- Comparison Operators

- Lists

- Dictionaries

- The openpyxl Library, Classes, & Objects

- Loop (Bfr counter)

- Read data from a Cell

- Loop (Aft counter)

- Search for a Match

- If ... Else Statements

2.1 Introduction

In this lab, I gather business expenses for my taxes. I have to assign a category to each expense and provide a "sum total" for each category. The source of each business expense is a filename in the "Receipts" directory. I add each filename to a Python "list" called "files." As I parse each filename into a date, description, and amount, I create a dictionary key:value pair. I also have an Excel file of phrases assigned to categories.

- Filenames: gather Date, Description, Amount, and Category from each filename

- Categorize each expense

- Create lists of expenses and sum totals for each category (for example, Advertising)

- Create a *Business Expenses.xlsx* with all the data

After assigning a category to a business expense, I add the amount to a running sum total for that category. For each business expense, I create a row in an "openpyxl" worksheet. Once I've categorized all expenses, I write each category sum total to the worksheet, as shown in the next example. I also create a separate worksheet for each category of expenses, such as "Advertising" or "Other." Finally, I format and save the worksheet.

	A	B	C	D
1		272.26	Advertising	
2		450.00	Professional	
3		50.50	Other	
4		31.31	Office Expense	
5		171.42	Assets	
6		37.45	Supplies	
7		50.40	Misc	
8				
9				
10	**Date**	**Amount**	**Description**	**Category**
11	01/02/20	272.26	AMZ Advertising	ADVERTISING
12	01/07/20	39.00	training	OTHER MISC EXPENSES
13	01/08/20	450.00	Professional services CPA	LEGAL & PROFESSIONAL
14	02/01/20	37.45	USB-C monitor cable	SUPPLIES
15	04/14/20	12.90	Coreldraw	OTHER PUBLISHING EXPENSES
16	04/17/20	31.31	Filing Storage boxes	OFFICE EXPENSES
17	05/05/20	9.99	research -Book	OTHER PUBLISHING EXPENSES
18	06/26/20	27.61	Book Proof	OTHER PUBLISHING EXPENSES
19	10/04/20	11.40	Editing	OTHER MISC EXPENSES
20	11/11/20	171.42	Apple store pencil, keyboard, ipad	ASSETS

Business_Expenses

Filenames

Each filename follows a similar pattern.

- The date of the expense.
- A description of the expense.
- The amount of the expense.

100420 Proof $11.40.eml

The next figure shows the files in the Finder app on my Mac.

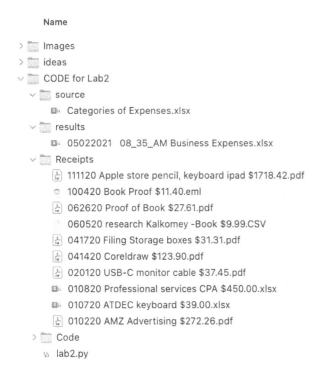

Name

> 📁 Images
> 📁 ideas
∨ 📁 CODE for Lab2
  ∨ 📁 source
    📊 Categories of Expenses.xlsx
  ∨ 📁 results
    📊 05022021 08_35_AM Business Expenses.xlsx
  ∨ 📁 Receipts
    📄 111120 Apple store pencil, keyboard ipad $1718.42.pdf
    ✉ 100420 Book Proof $11.40.eml
    📄 062620 Proof of Book $27.61.pdf
    📄 060520 research Kalkomey -Book $9.99.CSV
    📄 041720 Filing Storage boxes $31.31.pdf
    📄 041420 Coreldraw $123.90.pdf
    📄 020120 USB-C monitor cable $37.45.pdf
    📊 010820 Professional services CPA $450.00.xlsx
    📊 010720 ATDEC keyboard $39.00.xlsx
    📄 010220 AMZ Advertising $272.26.pdf
> 📁 Code
  📄 lab2.py

Figure 2.1   Lab 2 Files

2.2 Categories

Before I can submit my taxes, I need to categorize each expense. The Excel file "*Categories of Expenses.xlsx*" in the "source" directory has two columns of data, as shown below. I need to find the "Key Phrase" in the "filename" to assign the corresponding "Category."

Categories of Expenses.xlsx	
A	B
1 **Key Phrase**	**Category**
2 Advertising	Advertising

3	proof	Other Publishing Expenses
4	Apple Store	Decpreciation & Section 179
5	CPA	Legal & Professional
6	Book Proof	Other Publishing Expense
Sheet1		

This business expense belongs to the "Other Publishing Expenses" category.

100420 Proof $11.40.eml

2.3 The Program Pseudocode

Step 1. The first few lines in the *lab2.py* script update my computer's path to include a "code" subfolder and import modules or libraries. I've created six modules for tasks in this lab. Each module is a simple script file with one function.

- createCategoryDict.py
- getCategory.py
- getFilename.py
- writeSumTotalsToFile.py
- categoryWorksheets.py
- formatExcelFile.py

In addition to my modules, I'm using Python's built-in "string," "os," and "sys" modules, as well as the popular "openpyxl" library.

My *lab2.py* script also includes a function, **sumtotals()**, to update eight category objects. In this case, I thought it was easier to use global variables instead of importing a module and passing eight objects back and forth.

Step 2. Create a "Category" dictionary.

Step 3. Create float variables and lists for the "sum total" categories.

Step 4. Create worksheets for the output.

Step 5. Get a list of "filenames" in the "source" directory. If the filename begins with a number, go to the next step.

Step 6. Use slicing to get the "date" from the filename.

Step 7. Use slicing to get the "amount" from the filename.

Step 8. Use slicing to get the "description" from the filename.

Step 9. Assign the "date," "amount," and "description" to a worksheet object.

Step 10. Lookup the expense category

Step 11. Create a dictionary of the filename, date, amount, description, and category. If there is a category, go to step 12

Step 12. Add the business expense to the corresponding sum total for that category.

Step 13. Write the sum totals (sumAdv, sumProf, sumOther, sumDepr) to worksheet objects.

Step 14. Format the worksheet objects.

Step 15. Save the output file.

Step 16. As a sanity check, print the total number of filenames and categories expenses to the Console.

3. Gather Data

In this chapter, we discuss

First Steps

Get a List of Filenames

Loop Through & Parse Filenames

The Output Worksheet Object

Get the Categories

Populate the Dictionary of Expenses

At this point, you should have Python installed, and you're ready to start coding. If you want to follow along with the script files, download the files from GitHub and create the file structure we looked at in Chapter 2.

\Main Folder\lab2.py

\Main Folder\Code*.py

\Main Folder\Source

\Main Foler\Results

This chapter focuses on **Steps 1-9**. For each line, I'll explain the logic behind the code, as well as the syntax. For now, I'm going to briefly mention the "sumtotal" module and output functions since I cover them in later chapters. You might think of the first few lines of code as "prep" work. I'm also creating the lists and dictionaries I'll use later.

- Set up the environment in **Step 1**.

- Also, in **Step 1**, load the lab modules.

- Finally, **Step 1** creates the sumTotal() function.

- Create list and dictionary variables in **Steps 2-3**.

- Create workbook and worksheet objects for the output in **Step 4**.

- The main body of the program begins on line 96 with **Step 5**. After gathering a list of filenames from the "source" folder, the code loops through the filenames to gather data.

- Lines 105-118 are **Steps 6-8** and use slicing to extract the "date," "amount," and "description" from each filename.

- In **Step 9**, lines 120-122 assign the "date," "amount," and "description" to cells in the openpyxl worksheet object. We'll look at lines 124-131 in the next chapter on categories. Finally, I create a dictionary named expenses_Dict with the data I've collected.

3.1 First Steps

The first few lines in the *lab2.py* script update my computer's path to include a "code" subfolder. This is **Step 1**. I must update the path before I can import the modules for Lab 2.

lab2.py

```
1   import string
2   from openpyxl import Workbook
3   import os
4   import sys
5   currentWorkingDir = os.getcwd()
6   codeDir = currentWorkingDir + '/code'
7
8   sys.path.insert(0, codeDir)
9
```

```
10
11    # these modules are in the /code subdirectory
12    from createCategoryDict import createCategoryDict
13    from getCategory import getCategory
14    from getFilename import getFilename
15    from writeSumTotalsToFile import writeSumTotalsToFile
16    from formatExcelFile import formatExcelFile
17    from categoryWorksheets import categoryWorksheets
18
```

Update the Path

In case you want to store some modules in a different directory, lines 5-8 demonstrate how to add to your computer's path. Because I'm using a Mac, line 6 has a forward slash. On a Windows machine, use backslashes.

lab2.py

```
5    currentWorkingDir = os.getcwd()
6    codeDir = currentWorkingDir + '/code'
7
8    sys.path.insert(0, codeDir)
```

Import Modules

Before you can use an external module (*.py file) in *lab2.py*, you have to "import" the module. Lines 1-4 and 12-17 import various modules or libraries. In addition to my six lab modules, on lines 1-4, I import Python's built-in "string," "os," and "sys" modules, as well as the popular "openpyxl" library.

- createCategoryDict.py
- getCategory.py
- getFilename.py
- writeSumTotalsToFile.py
- categoryWorksheets.py
- formatExcelFile.py

lab2.py

```
1    import string
2    from openpyxl import Workbook
3    import os
4    import sys
5    currentWorkingDir = os.getcwd()
6    codeDir = currentWorkingDir + '/code'
7
8    sys.path.insert(0, codeDir)
9
10
11   # these modules are in the /code subdirectory
12   from createCategoryDict import createCategoryDict
13   from getCategory import getCategory
14   from getFilename import getFilename
15   from writeSumTotalsToFile import writeSumTotalsToFile
16   from formatExcelFile import formatExcelFile
17   from categoryWorksheets import categoryWorksheets
18
```

My *lab2.py* script also includes a function, **sumtotals**(), to update fourteen category objects. In this case, I thought it was easier to use global variables in the function instead of importing a module and passing fourteen objects back and forth.

> The "Python Basics" chapter has information on global variables, as well as memory, namespace, global scope, and local scope.

In the next chapter, we'll look at the **sumtotals**() function in detail, along with the **createCategoryDict**() and **getCategory**() functions. In Chapter 6 we'll use the last four lab functions shown below .

getFilename()

writeSumTotalsToFile()

formatExcelFile()

categoryWorksheets()

Create the Output Filename

To demonstrate adding a timestamp to your filename, I import the **getFilename**() function on line 14 of the *lab2.py*. Essentially **getFilename**() just creates a filename with a path for the output file.

	getFilename.py
14	def getFilename():
15	from datetime import datetime
16	import os
17	
18	mypath = os.environ['HOME']
19	mypath += '/BOOK_AUTHORING/Python_Lab2/CODE_for_Lab2/results/'
20	d1 = datetime.strftime(datetime.now(), '%m%d%Y %H_%M_%p')
21	return mypath + d1 + ' Business Expenses.xlsx'

In the *getFilename.py* file, line 15 imports the "datetime" library and function of the same name, **.datetime**. Line 16 imports the "os" library, and line 18 uses the "os" library method **.environ** to get my computer's **home** directory.

Line 20 retrieves the date and time with the **.now**() function from the "datetime" library. Line 20 also uses the **.strftime**() function to format the value as a string object.

The **getFilename**() function returns a string object on line 21, as shown below. The wb.**save**() method expects a filename with path as a string parameter

/BOOK_AUTHORING/Python_Lab2/CODE_for_Lab2/results/ 05292021   07_42_AM Business Expenses.xlsx

To demonstrate using the **.save** method, on line 157 in the *lab2.py* file, I save the "wb" object again with a different filename. Essentially I create two identical workbooks with different names.

Define a Function

Lines 19-37 are comments about the **sumTotals**() function defined on line 38. I call the **sumtotals**() function on line 130 when we're working on categories. We'll look at this function in detail in the next chapter.

	lab2.py
38	def **sumTotals**(category, thisAmt, tempList):
39	global sumAdv, sumOther, sumProf, sumOffice
40	global sumSupplies, sumMisc, sumAssets

```
41          global advList, otherList, profList, miscList
42          global officeList, assetsList, suppliesList
43
44          if category == 'ADVERTISING':
45              sumAdv += float(thisAmt)
46              advList.append(tempList)
47          elif category == 'LEGAL & PROFESSIONAL':
48              sumProf += float(thisAmt)
49              profList.append(tempList)
50          elif category == 'OTHER PUBLISHING EXPENSES':
51              sumOther += float(thisAmt)
52              otherList.append(tempList)
53          elif category == 'OFFICE EXPENSES':
54              sumOffice += float(thisAmt)
55              officeList.append(tempList)
56          elif category == 'ASSETS':
57              sumAssets += float(thisAmt)
58              assetsList.append(tempList)
59          elif category == 'SUPPLIES':
60              sumSupplies += float(thisAmt)
61              suppliesList.append(tempList)
62          elif category == 'OTHER MISC EXPENSES':
63              sumMisc += float(thisAmt)
64              miscList.append(tempList)
```

Create Float Variables

On lines 67 and 68 of the *lab2.py* file, I create float variables for the seven "sum total" category values. This is **Step 3.** The next chapter looks at the **sumTotals**() function in depth.

lab2.py

```
67  sumAdv, sumOther, sumProf, sumMisc = 0.0, 0.0, 0.0, 0.0
68  sumOffice, sumAssets, sumSupplies = 0.0, 0.0, 0.0
```

Create Category Expense Lists

For each category, I also create a list for the expense details on lines 69 and 70. There are seven lists, as shown below. In the next chapter, I'll add data to these lists.

These seven lists have the data I'll use to create seven Excel worksheets, as shown in Chapter 6.

```
                              lab2.py
69  advList, otherList, profList, miscList = [], [], [], []
70  officeList, assetsList, suppliesList = [], [], []
```

Create the Category Dictionary

The Excel file "*Categories of Expenses.xlsx*" has two columns of data, as shown below. I need to find the "Key Phrase" in the "Filename" to assign the corresponding "Category." This is **Step 2** and is covered in detail in the next chapter.

	A	B
1	**Key Phrase**	**Category**
2	Advertising	Advertising
3	proof	Other Publishing Expenses
4	Apple Store	Decpreciation & Section 179
5	CPA	Legal & Professional
6	Book Proof	Other Publishing Expense
Sheet1		

On line 73, I create an empty dictionary. On line 74, the **createCategoryDict()** function returns a dictionary that is assigned to the **expCategories_Dict** object.

```
                              lab2.py
73  expCategories_Dict = {}
74  expCategories_Dict = createCategoryDict()
75
```

Create a Worksheet for the Output

In **Step 4**, lines 78-80 create a worksheet "Business_Expenses" for the output. On line 77, I set the **row_out** variable to "11" so that I begin writing expense detailed data to row eleven of the worksheet object.

```
                              lab2.py
77  row_out = 11
78  wb = Workbook()
79  ws = wb.create_sheet('Business_Expenses')
80  wb.remove(wb['Sheet'])
```

At the end of the program, I save the workbook "wb" object as "*Business_Expenses.xlsx.*" A sample of the "Business_Expenses.xlsx" is shown below. The **categoryWorksheets**() function also creates seven worksheets for each category of expenses. We'll look at categories and output in the next chapters.

	A	B	C	D
1		272.26	Advertising	
2		450.00	Professional	
3		50.50	Other	
4		31.31	Office Expense	
5		171.42	Assets	
6		37.45	Supplies	
7		50.40	Misc	
8				
9				
10	**Date**	**Amount**	**Description**	**Category**
11	01/02/20	272.26	AMZ Advertising	ADVERTISING
12	01/07/20	39.00	training	OTHER MISC EXPENSES
13	01/08/20	450.00	Professional services CPA	LEGAL & PROFESSIONAL
14	02/01/20	37.45	USB-C monitor cable	SUPPLIES

Business_Expenses

After I write column 4 to the "ws" worksheet object on line 131, I increment the "**row_out**" counter on line 132. We'll look at lines 96-134 in detail in the topic, "3.3 Loop Through Filenames" that follows.

```
                              lab2.py
127         if not thisCategory:
128             print("Couldn't find category for:", thisFileName)
```

```
129            else:
130                 sumTotals(thisCategory, thisAmt, tempList)
131                 ws.cell(row_out, 4).value = thisCategory
132            row_out += 1
133
134            expenses_Dict[thisFileName] = tempList
```

Create a Dictionary for Business Expenses

On line 83, I create an empty dictionary for the business expenses. As I loop through rows in the worksheet object, I add data to the **expenses_Dict** dictionary. The topic "3.6 Populate the Dictionary of Expenses" explains how to add data to this dictionary.

Step 11. Create a dictionary of the filename, date, amount, description, and category. If there is a category, go to Step 12.

```
                          lab2.py
83   expenses_Dict = {}
```

The dictionary key is the filename, and the value is a list of these four elements.

- thisDate
- thisDesc
- thisAmt
- thisCategory

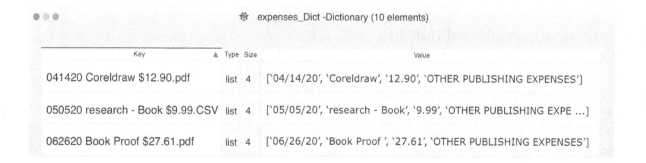

Figure 3.1   The expenses_Dict

Create a String of Numbers

On line 86, I create a string of the numbers 0-9. My naming convention for filenames is the filename begins with a number. I use this "numbers" list later on line 99 to verify the filename begins with a number.

lab2.py
86 numbers = string.digits

3.2 Get a List of Filenames

To gather the filenames in the "source" directory, line 92 uses the **.listdir** method from the "os" library to create a list of filenames called "files." This is the beginning of **Step 5**. A sample of the "files" list showing three elements follows. Notice the filename is a "string" type.

files - List (11 elements)			
Index ▲	Type	Size	Value
0	str	27	041420 Coreldraw $12.90.pdf
1	str	31	050520 research - Book $9.99.CSV
2	str	28	062620 Book Proof $27.61.pdf

Figure 3.2   The files List

Line 92 also demonstrates how to use the **sorted**() function to sort a list. While not necessary for this lab, I thought I'd demonstrate sorting.

```
                            lab2.py
89  mypath1 = os.environ['HOME']
90  mypath2 = os.path.join(mypath1, 'BOOK_AUTHORING', 'Python_Lab2',
91                         'Code_for_Lab2', 'Receipts')
92  files = sorted(os.listdir(mypath2))
93
```

3.3 Loop Through & Parse Filenames

The main body of the program begins on line 96 with a "for loop" that ends on line 134. Lines 96-134 are a "suite" or "block" of code. A suite begins with a control statement and includes all the indented lines of code that follow. The control statement on line 96 iterates through all the filenames in "files." The statements to parse the filename into variables run from lines 97-134. The code then loops back to line 96 to repeat executing lines 97-134 for the next filename.

	lab2.py
96	for i in range(len(files)):
97	thisFileName = str(files[i])
98	lenFileName = len(thisFileName)
99	if thisFileName[0] in numbers:
100	thisDate, thisDesc, thisCategory = '', '', ''
101	tempList = []
102	dollarSignIndex, end, thisAmt = 0, 0, 0.0
103	
104	
105	thisDate += thisFileName[:2]
106	thisDate += r'/'
107	thisDate += thisFileName[2:4]
108	thisDate += r'/'
109	thisDate += thisFileName[4:6]

On line 100, I create the variables I use when I parse "thisFileName." Because I want the variables to be empty each time I parse a new filename, I create the variables within the "for loop" that begins on line 96 and ends on line 134. Line 100 creates three blank string variables.

- thisDate
- thisDesc
- thisCategory

An empty list called "tempList" is created on line 101. Later I'll add the three variables to "tempList." Line 102 creates the float variable thisAmt and assigns the value 0.0.

- tempList
- thisAmt

Parse Filenames

On lines 105-118, I parse the filename into three string elements.

- Date
- Description
- Amount

For each filename, I want to find three values: the date, description, and amount. These three variables represent this data.

- thisDate
- thisDescription
- thisAmt

As I parse the filename, I do not include the dollar sign or the extension suffix. On line 112, I search for the "index" of the '$' character and assign that index to the variable "dollarSignIndex." On line 113, I assign the variable "end" to the '.' period index. In effect, line 114 is dropping the filename extension.

Finally, I create a "list" with the three string variables, as shown below. Each filename is parsed into a similar list.

[thisDate, thisDesc, thisAmt]

Let's look at a sample filename from the "files" list. Because it is enclosed in quotes, it is a string object.

'100420 Proof $11.40.eml'

After I parse the filename into three variables, I create a list that contains these three variables. Commas separate the list elements. The entire "list" is enclosed in square brackets, indicating it is a list. Using the filename example, the three variables in the list would represent the values shown below.

['100420', 'Proof', '11.40']

In the topics that follow, I parse the filename using slicing, passing a start and stop value to indicate the locations within the string.

```
                              lab2.py
96  for i in range(len(files)):
97       thisFileName = str(files[i])
98       lenFileName = len(thisFileName)
99       if thisFileName[0] in numbers:
100          thisDate, thisDesc, thisCategory = '', '', ''
101          tempList = []
102          dollarSignIndex, end, thisAmt = 0, 0, 0.0
103
104
105          thisDate += thisFileName[:2]
106          thisDate += r'/'
107          thisDate += thisFileName[2:4]
108          thisDate += r'/'
109          thisDate += thisFileName[4:6]
110
111          if '$' in thisFileName:
112              dollarSignIndex = thisFileName.rindex('$') + 1
113              end = thisFileName.rindex('.')
114              thisAmt = thisFileName[dollarSignIndex:end]
115          else:
116              print('No $ Amount in Filename', thisFileName)
117
118          thisDesc = thisFileName[7:dollarSignIndex - 1]
```

Get the Date

In **Step 6**, I use **slicing** to tokenize the filename. Slicing takes a sequence and breaks it into a substring of elements based on a "start" end "stop" value. While slicing takes three arguments separated by colons, here I am using only the start and stop arguments.

thisFileName[start:stop:step]

Start defaults to 0, and "step" defaults to 1. Both start and step are optional keyword arguments. If only one argument is given, it is used as the "stop" argument. The default for the second argument, "stop," is the length of the object, in this case, .

The first six characters of my filename represent the month-day-year. Python begins counting indices at 0, so in this example, the date is found at indices 0-5. The day "**04**" is index 2 and 3, as shown below.

						100420 Proof $11.40.eml																
1	0	**0**	**4**	2	0		P	r	o	o	f		$	1	1	.	4	0	.	e	m	l
0	1	2	3	4	5	6	7	8	9	10	11	12	13	14	15	16	17	18	19	20	21	22

What happens on line 105 for this example, where the month of October is "10?" Because there is no "start" argument, Python uses the default or "0." Since only one value, [:**2**], is given, Python knows it is the stop argument. For the stop argument thisFileName[:**2**], Python returns the characters at index 0 and 1. In effect, Python stops before "2."

In this example, the day is "**04**" and begins at index "2" and stops before index "4," as shown on line 107. As I gather the month, day, and year, I add slashes between the strings on lines 106 and 108.

```
                                    lab2.py
100        thisDate, thisDesc, thisCategory = '', '', ''
101        tempList = []
102        dollarSignIndex, end, thisAmt = 0, 0, 0.0
103
104
105        thisDate += thisFileName[:2]
106        thisDate += r'/'
107        thisDate += thisFileName[2:4]
108        thisDate += r'/'
109        thisDate += thisFileName[4:6]
```

Get the Amount

In **Step 7**, I find the amount in the filename. In this example, the amount is the characters at index 14-18.

> Although the amount is after the "description" in the filename, I need the index location of the "$" dollar sign to identify the end of the description. For this reason, I gather the description, or **Step 8**, after the amount.

	100420 Proof $11.40.eml																					
1	0	0	4	2	0		P	r	o	o	f		$	1	1	.	4	0	.	e	m	l
0	1	2	3	4	5	6	7	8	9	10	11	12	13	14	15	16	17	18	19	20	21	22

Looking at the example below, on line 111, I test if the dollar sign '$' character is in the filename. If line 111 evaluates to "True," lines 112-116 are executed.

In line 112, the string method **.rindex()** searches from the right side of the filename string to find the '$' character. In this example, line 112 returns the index "13." Because I want slicing to start after the dollar sign, I add "1" to the index on line 112. My "start" argument for slicing is, therefore, 14 and is assigned to the variable "dollarSignIndex."

I want to stop slicing at the last period or '.' character in the filename. Line 113 also uses the **.rindex()** method to find the last period in the filename, which is index 19. The "end" variable is assigned to "19."

```
dollarSignIndex = 14
end = 19
```

The slicing on line 114 is equivalent to the statement below, which evaluates to "**11.40**." If line 111 evaluates to "False," the Python Interpreter moves to the "**else**" statement that begins on like 115 and prints a message out to the Console.

```
thisAmt = thisFileName[14:19]
```

	lab2.py
111	if '$' in thisFileName:
112	dollarSignIndex = thisFileName.rindex('$') + 1

```
113              end = thisFileName.rindex('.')
114              thisAmt = thisFileName[dollarSignIndex:end]
115          else:
116              print('No $ Amount in Filename', thisFileName)
```

Get the Description

In **Step 8**, I find the "description" in the filename. Index "7" is always the beginning of the description in my filename.

In this example, the description is at index 7-11.

100420 Proof $11.40.eml																							
1	0	0	4	2	0		**P**	**r**	**o**	**o**	**f**		$	1	1	.	4	0	.	e	m	l
0	1	2	3	4	5	6	7	8	9	10	11	12	13	14	15	16	17	18	19	20	21	22

Earlier, we found '$" at index "13" and assigned "14" to "dollarSignIndex." The statement below returns "**Proof** " with an extra space at the end.

thisFileName[7:dollarSignIndex]

Because all my filenames follow the same naming convention, I can remove the space at the end by subtracting "1" from the index. Line 118 is the equivalent of this expression, which evaluates to "**Proof**" with no trailing whitespace.

thisFileName[7:14-1]

lab2.py
```
118          thisDesc = thisFileName[7:dollarSignIndex - 1]
```

> If the format of your string varies so that you don't know the exact beginning or end of letters, the string methods **.strip()** and **.rstrip()** also remove whitespace characters.

3.4 The Output Worksheet Object

On lines 120-122, I write the date, amount, and description to the "ws" object or the worksheet "Business_Expenses." Earlier, on line 77, I set the **row_out** variable to "11" so that I begin writing data to row eleven. Starting at row eleven allows for the sum totals in rows 1-7 and the headings in row 10.

	lab2.py
120	ws.cell(row_out, 1).value = thisDate
121	ws.cell(row_out, 2).value = float(thisAmt)
122	ws.cell(row_out, 3).value = thisDesc

	A	B	C	D
11	01/02/20	272.26	AMZ Advertising	ADVERTISING
12	01/07/20	39.00	training	OTHER MISC EXPENSES
Business_Expenses				

3.5 Get the Categories

The next chapter goes into detail for the **getCategory**() function, but I'll provide a brief summary here. In the *lab2.py* script on line 124, I call the **getCategory()** function from the *getCategory.py* file. The **getCategory()** function takes the filename, looks up the category in the **expCategories_Dict**, and returns a category in the string variable "thisCategory." The statement on line 124 assigns the return value from the getCategory() function to "thisCategory."

	lab2.py
124	thisCategory = getCategory(thisFileName, expCategories_Dict)
125	tempList = [thisDate, thisDesc, thisAmt, thisCategory]

Note that earlier line 100 created three blank strings.

- thisDate
- thisDesc
- thisCategory

Line 102 creates the float variable thisAmt and assigns the value 0.0.

- thisAmt

After line 124 retrieves the "category," I have values for all four variables. On line 125, I assign the four variables to "tempList." Earlier I created an empty list called "tempList" on line 101.

- tempList

3.6 Populate the Dictionary of Expenses

Now that I have a list of values, on line 134, I add the "tempList" data to a dictionary called "**expenses_Dict**." The **expenses_Dict** key is the filename, and the value is the tempList that contains the four elements:

- thisDate
- thisDesc
- thisAmt
- thisCategory

The layout for the dictionary **expenses_Dict** is shown below, where "thisFileName" is the dictionary key.

expenses_Dict[thisFileName] = [thisDate, thisDesc, thisAmt, thisCategory]

Earlier, we talked about the "tempList" object. On line 125, I created a "tempList" object for the parsed filename's data.

lab2.py
```
125        tempList = [thisDate, thisDesc, thisAmt, thisCategory]
```

I use "tempList" on line 130 when I'm updating sum totals and again on line 134 when I create a new object in the **expenses_Dict**. Because it is a list, the values are enclosed in square brackets, as shown below.

> tempList = **[**thisDate, thisDesc, thisAmt, thisCategory**]**

At this point there are only three elements in the list; however, I add the category as the fourth element in the next step.

We look at the **sumTotals**() function in detail in the next chapter.

```
                               lab2.py
125          tempList = [thisDate, thisDesc, thisAmt, thisCategory]
126
127      if not thisCategory:
128          print("Couldn't find category for:", thisFileName)
129      else:
130          sumTotals(thisCategory, thisAmt, tempList)
131          ws.cell(row_out, 4).value = thisCategory
132      row_out += 1
133
134      expenses_Dict[thisFileName] = tempList
```

A Python "dictionary" is similar to a phone book, and searches are very fast. A Python dictionary has "keys" and corresponding "values."

4. Categorize Data

In this Chapter, we discuss

Create the Category Dictionary

Get the Categories for Each Expense

The Category Lists & Floats

The sumTotals( ) Function

Match Categories

Add Expenses to the Sum Total Variables

Append to the Category Lists

In this Chapter, we assign categories to each business expense, add amounts to sum totals, and finally create the category lists.

- Create a dictionary from the Excel file "*Categories of Expenses.xlsx*" and assign phrases to each category. This dictionary is named **expCategories_Dict**.

- For each "filename," look up the expense category.

- Add expense amounts to the corresponding "category sum total."

- Add expense details to the corresponding category list.

4.1 Create the Category Dictionary

The Excel file "Categories of Expenses.xlsx" in the "source" directory has two columns of data, as shown below. I want to find the "Key Phrase" in the "filename" to assign the corresponding "Category." This is **Step 2**.

	A	B
	Key Phrase	Category
1		
2	Advertising	Advertising
3	proof	Other Publishing Expenses
4	Apple Store	Decpreciation & Section 179
5	CPA	Legal & Professional
6	Book Proof	Other Publishing Expense

Sheet1

On line 73, I create an empty underlined dictionary called **expCategories_Dict**. In the *lab2.py* script on line 74, I call the **createCategoryDict**() function and assign the return object to **expCategories_Dict**.

After the function call on line 74, the Python interpreter moves into the code in the *createCategory_Dict.py* file. After the code in the *createCategory_Dict.py* file runs, the Python interpreter moves back to the *lab2.py* file.

Chapter 3 looked at line 12 of the *lab2.py* that imports the **createCategoryDict**() function from the *createCategoryDict.py* file.

```
                                lab2.py
73  expCategories_Dict = {}
74  expCategories_Dict = createCategoryDict()
```

The comments on lines 1-7 in the *createCategory_Dict.py* file explain what the function returns. The function definition for **createCategoryDict**() begins on line 10, as shown below.

```
                              createCategoryDict.py
10  def createCategoryDict():
11        from openpyxl import load_workbook
12        import os
13
14        codeDir = os.getcwd()
15        source = codeDir + "/source/"
16        filename = source + "Categories of Expenses.xlsx"
17
18        wbCategories = load_workbook(filename, data_only=True)
19        wsCategories = wbCategories["Sheet1"]
20
21        expCategories_Dict = {}
22        phrase, category = '', ''
23
24        for row in range(2, wsCategories.max_row + 1):
25            phrase = wsCategories.cell(row, 1).value
26            phrase = phrase.upper()
27            category = wsCategories.cell(row, 2).value.upper()
28            expCategories_Dict[phrase] = category
29
30        return expCategories_Dict
```

Add Directory to the Path

Because the Excel file "Categories of Expenses.xlsx" is in the "source" directory, I need to add the "source" directory to my computer's path.

On line 12, I import the "os" library, and then I call the **getcwd**() function on line 14 to get the current working directory. On lines 15-16, I create a string with the path and filename.

Because I am running this code on my Mac, I use backslashes on line 15. If you're using a Windows machine, use forward slashes on line 15.

createCategoryDict.py

```
10   def createCategoryDict():
11        from openpyxl import load_workbook
12        import os
13
14        codeDir = os.getcwd()
15        source = codeDir + "/source/"
16        filename = source + "Categories of Expenses.xlsx"
```

Create the Workbook and Worksheet Objects

On line 11, I import the **.load_workbook** method from the "openpyxl" library. On line 18, I call the **.load_workbook** method to create the object "wbCategories" for the *"Categories of Expenses.xlsx"* workbook. Since I'm not going to change the data in the worksheet, I use the **data_only=True** parameter in the function call.

createCategoryDict.py

```
10   def createCategoryDict():
11        from openpyxl import load_workbook
12        import os
13
14        codeDir = os.getcwd()
15        source = codeDir + "/source/"
16        filename = source + "Categories of Expenses.xlsx"
17
18        wbCategories = load_workbook(filename, data_only=True)
19        wsCategories = wbCategories["Sheet1"]
```

On line 18, the openpyxl library method **.load_workbook** loads data from the workbook *"Categories of Expenses.xlsx."* On line 19, I assign the "wsCategories" variable to the **wbCategories['Sheet1']** object.

Loop Through Rows

In Python, the first line of a <u>control statement</u>, and all the indented lines that follow, are called a "Suite" of code. In the next figure, there is a shaded box around the code from line 24 to line 28. I added a red vertical dotted line to highlight the control statement.

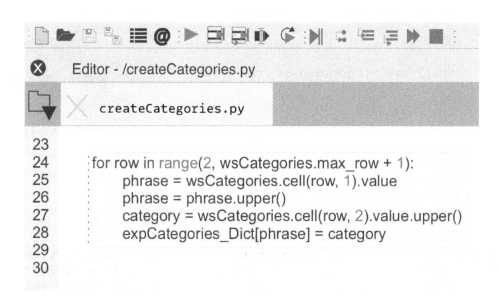

Figure 4.1   createCategoryDict.py "for loop"

This "for loop" begins on line 24 and iterates over the worksheet rows starting at row 2 and ending at row 10. Each time through the "for loop," I gather the "phrase" and "category" and then move on to the next row.

Column 1 = phrase

Column 2 = category

The first row in the worksheet has headings, so I begin reading the data on row 2. The **range**() function takes two parameters, start and stop, and is similar to "slicing" that we looked at in Chapter 3. The range() parameters on line 24 evaluate to:

range(2,11)

The openpyxl method **.max_row** returns the number of the last row with data, in this case, 10. On line 19, I created the wsCategories object for the Excel worksheet data. The syntax to get the "max_row" for the wsCategories object is:

wsCategories.**max_row**

The **range**() function stops before the "stop" value, so I add "1" to the max_row return value.

$$range(2, wsCategories.max\_row + 1)$$

For example, if I have ten rows in my worksheet, my "stop" value should be 11, or **range**(2, 11).

Gather Data

In the *createCategoryDict.py* script file, the "row" variable begins at row 2 and increases by one each time through the loop. For example, the first time through the loop, the value for A2 is "Advertising" because the **range** function began on row "2." The second time through the loop row=3, and the value for A3 is "proof." Inside the "for loop," four statements gather data, modify data, and add data to the **expCategories_Dict**.

- Get the phrase.
- Change the "phrase" to uppercase.
- Get the "uppercase" category on line 27.
- Create a key value:pair in the expCategories_Dict.

createCategoryDict.py

```
24      for row in range(2, wsCategories.max_row + 1):
25          phrase = wsCategories.cell(row, 1).value
26          phrase = phrase.upper()
27          category = wsCategories.cell(row, 2).value.upper()
28          expCategories_Dict[phrase] = category
```

On line 25, I use the openpyxl method **.cell**() to return the value in column 1, or the "phrase." The **.cell**() method also accepts the following syntax.

$$ws.cell(row=row\_out, column=1).value$$

On line 26, I convert the "phrase" string to uppercase to make matching strings easier. For the "category," I gather the data from column 2 and convert the string to uppercase in one statement. On line 27, I change the value in wsCategories.cell(row,2).value to uppercase, and assign the value to variable "category." Finally, to speed up searches, on line 28, I add "phrase" and "category" to a Python dictionary called "**expCategories_Dict**."

createCategoryDict.py

```
27          category = wsCategories.cell(row, 2).value.upper()
28          expCategories_Dict[phrase] = category
```

The "phrase" is the dictionary key, and the "category" is the value. If you're not familiar with dictionaries, the "Python Basics" chapter has additional information on creating and updating dictionaries.

expCategories_Dict[phrase] = category

Figure 4.2   expCategories_Dict

> A Python dictionary is similar to a phone book, and searches are very fast. So, for example, if the dictionary key is a "name," the dictionary value is a "phone number."

4.2 Get the Categories for each expense

In the *lab2.py* script on line 124, I call the **getCategory**() function, which returns a string variable "thisCategory." This is **Step 10**.

lab2.py

```
124            thisCategory = getCategory(thisFileName, expCategories_Dict)
125            tempList = [thisDate, thisDesc, thisAmt, thisCategory]
```

Chapter 3 looked at line 13 of the *lab2.py*, which imports this **getCategory**() function from the *getCategory.py* file.

The **getCategory**() function checks if a "phrase" from the **expCategories_Dict** is **in** the filename on line 17, as shown below. The **expCategories_Dict** dictionary keys are the phrases. Looking at line 29, you can see how this statement returns the value of the dictionary key:value pair.

expCategories_Dict[phrase]

Let's look at the *getCategory.py* file code in detail. The function definition for **getCategory**() begins on line 15. Line 16 creates an empty <u>string</u> variable named "thisCategory." Lines 17 creates a loop to iterate through every key in the **expCategories_Dict**.

getCategory.py

```
15  def getCategory(thisFileName, expCategories_Dict):
16      thisCategory = ''
17      for phrase in expCategories_Dict:
18          if phrase in thisFileName.upper():
19              thisCategory = expCategories_Dict[phrase]
20              return thisCategory
21      return thisCategory
```

When the "phrase" is found in the "filename" on line 18, the program runs line 19, and then line 20 immediately returns the value. If there are a lot of values in the **expCategories_Dict,** performance improves dramatically because the loop ends after a match. If the loop ends and there is no match, line 21 returns the original value from line 16. Without a return statement on line 21, the function returns the value "None."

Note, I could have combined lines 18 and 19 into a single statement, as shown below.

	getCategory.py
19	return expCategories_Dict[phrase]

Update tempList

Now that I extracted these four values from the filename, I create a "tempList" of values on line 125 in *lab2.py*, as shown below.

- Date
- Description
- Amount
- Category

	lab2.py
125	tempList = [thisDate, thisDesc, thisAmt, thisCategory]
126	
127	if not thisCategory and not thisAmt:
128	print("Couldn't find category or amount for:", thisFileName)
129	else:
130	sumTotals(thisCategory, thisAmt, tempList)
131	ws.cell(row_out, 4).value = thisCategory
132	row_out += 1

In the next topic, we'll look at the category lists and float variables for the function **sumtotals**(). The **sumtotals**() function called on line 130 takes "**tempList**" as an argument, then adds "tempList" data to the corresponding category list and float variable.

4.3 The Category Lists & Floats

For each of the seven categories of business expenses, I create variables for two types of data. There are a total of fourteen variables.

- sum total float variables
- category lists

Float Variables

Earlier I said I wanted a sum total for each category of expenses. As shown below, lines 67 and 68 create seven <u>float</u> variables to keep track of the sum total for each category. This is **Step 3**.

- sumAdv
- sumProf
- sumOther
- sumOffice
- sumAssets
- sumSupplies
- sumMisc

lab2.py

```
67  sumAdv, sumOther, sumProf, sumMisc = 0.0, 0.0, 0.0, 0.0
68  sumOffice, sumAssets, sumSupplies = 0.0, 0.0, 0.0
```

In a bit, we'll look at the **sumTotals**() <u>function</u> that converts the string "amount" to a float and adds the amount to the appropriate float variable. Ultimately, I'll write these seven sum total variables to the output Excel worksheet called 'Business_Expenses," as shown below.

	A	B	C
1		272.26	Advertising
2		450.00	Professional
3		50.50	Other
4		31.31	Office Expense
5		171.42	Assets
6		37.45	Supplies
7		50.40	Misc
8			

Business_Expenses

Category Lists

For each category, in **Step 3**, I create a list for expense details. In the next code example, this is lines 69 and 70.

```
                                    lab2.py
69  advList, otherList, profList, miscList = [], [], [], []
70  officeList, assetsList, suppliesList = [], [], []
```

- advList
- profList
- otherList
- officeList
- assetsList
- suppliesList
- miscList

Each category list contains "<u>list</u>" elements (nested lists), with data from each "filename." The "otherList" with three list elements is shown in the next diagram.

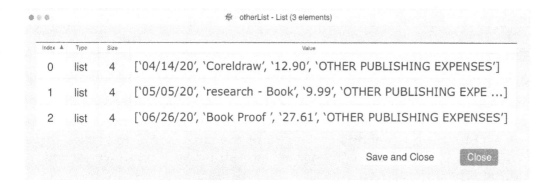

Index ▲	Type	Size	Value
0	list	4	['04/14/20', 'Coreldraw', '12.90', 'OTHER PUBLISHING EXPENSES']
1	list	4	['05/05/20', 'research - Book', '9.99', 'OTHER PUBLISHING EXPE ...']
2	list	4	['06/26/20', 'Book Proof ', '27.61', 'OTHER PUBLISHING EXPENSES']

Figure 4.3   The otherList

These seven lists have the data I use to create seven "category" Excel worksheets, as shown below. We'll look at creating these worksheets in the next Chapter.

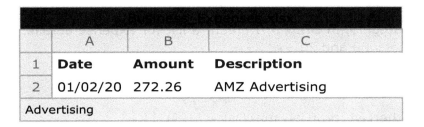

	A	B	C
1	**Date**	**Amount**	**Description**
2	01/02/20	272.26	AMZ Advertising

Advertising

4.4 The sumTotals() Function

The <u>function</u> **sumtotals**() updates two objects in each category. There is no return statement because the function updates global objects within the lab2.py file. The function definition runs from line 38 to line 64. The **sumTotals**() code does not run until I make the function call on line 130.

- The corresponding **sum total** float variable for the expense category. This is **Step 12**.

- The corresponding **category list** with details of the expense. This is **Step 13**.

> The "Python Basics" chapter has information on global variables, memory, namespace, global scope, and local scope.

SumTotals() Parameters

The **sumTotals**() function is defined on line 38 of the *lab2.py* file and takes three string parameters. Earlier, I parsed each "filename" into string variables. We looked at this in Chapter 3 in the topic, "Parse Filenames."

- category

- thisAmt

- tempList

```
38  def sumTotals(category, thisAmt, tempList):
```

For each "filename", I pass three variables when I call the **sumTotals**() function on line 130 of the *lab2.py* file.

lab2.py

```
130             sumTotals(thisCategory, thisAmt, tempList)
```

4.5 Match Categories

The if...elif statements on lines 44-64 test for a category match. When the "if" statement is "True," the next two lines update the category variables for that category. For example, line 45 updates the "sumAdv" float variable when the category is "ADVERTISING." Line 46 appends the "tempList" to "advList" when the category is "ADVERTISING."

lab2.py

```
38  def sumTotals(category, thisAmt, tempList):
39      global sumAdv, sumOther, sumProf, sumOffice
40      global sumSupplies, sumMisc, sumAssets
41      global advList, otherList, profList, miscList
42      global officeList, assetsList, suppliesList
43
44      if category == 'ADVERTISING':
45          sumAdv += float(thisAmt)
46          advList.append(tempList)
47      elif category == 'LEGAL & PROFESSIONAL':
48          sumProf += float(thisAmt)
49          profList.append(tempList)
50      elif category == 'OTHER PUBLISHING EXPENSES':
51          sumOther += float(thisAmt)
52          otherList.append(tempList)
53      elif category == 'OFFICE EXPENSES':
54          sumOffice += float(thisAmt)
55          officeList.append(tempList)
```

```
56        elif category == 'ASSETS':
57            sumAssets += float(thisAmt)
58            assetsList.append(tempList)
59        elif category == 'SUPPLIES':
60            sumSupplies += float(thisAmt)
61            suppliesList.append(tempList)
62        elif category == 'OTHER MISC EXPENSES':
63            sumMisc += float(thisAmt)
64            miscList.append(tempList)
```

4.6 Add Expenses to the Sum Totals

Within the main body of the program on line 130, I call the **sumTotals**() function and pass three variables.

lab2.py

```
125        tempList = [thisDate, thisDesc, thisAmt, thisCategory]
126
127        if not thisCategory and not thisAmt:
128            print("Couldn't find category or amount for:", thisFileName)
129        else:
130            sumTotals(thisCategory, thisAmt, tempList)
131            ws.cell(row_out, 4).value = thisCategory
132        row_out += 1
```

When the **sumTotals**() function finds a category match, it converts the amount from a "string" type to a "float" type. For example, line 45 converts "thisAmt" to a float, then adds "thisAmt" to "sumAdv."

lab2.py

```
38  def sumTotals(category, thisAmt, tempList):
39      global sumAdv, sumOther, sumProf, sumOffice
40      global sumSupplies, sumMisc, sumAssets
41      global advList, otherList, profList, miscList
42      global officeList, assetsList, suppliesList
43
44      if category == 'ADVERTISING':
```

| 45 | sumAdv += float(thisAmt) |
| 46 | advList.append(tempList) |

Using this filename as an example, let's walk through the **sumTotals**() function as it gathers the sum total amount.

100420 Proof $11.40.eml

As shown below, the function call on line 130 passes three parameters to the **sumTotals**() function. When Python executes line 130, the program moves up to the function definition on line 38 and runs the code from line 38 to 64.

- thisCategory
- thisAmt
- tempList

| | *lab2.py* |
| 130 | sumTotals(thisCategory, thisAmt, tempList) |

The values for this example are shown below.

```
thisAmt = 11.40
category = "OTHER PUBLISHING EXPENSES"
tempList = ['10/04/20', 'Editing', '11.40', 'OTHER MISC EXPENSES']
```

On line 51, I add the value of the string variable "thisAmt" to the float variable "sumOther." The function float(thisAmt) converts the string variable "thisAmt" to a float.

The **+=** operator adds the variable on the right side of the expression to the "sumOther" variable on the left side of the expression. For example, if sumOther = 50.00 before the statement, after line 51 runs sumOther = 61.40.

```
sumOther += float('11.40')
```

```
                              lab2.py
38  def sumTotals(category, thisAmt, tempList):
39          global sumAdv, sumOther, sumProf, sumOffice
40          global sumSupplies, sumMisc, sumAssets
41          global advList, otherList, profList, miscList
42          global officeList, assetsList, suppliesList
43
44          if category == 'ADVERTISING':
45              sumAdv += float(thisAmt)
46              advList.append(tempList)
47          elif category == 'LEGAL & PROFESSIONAL':
48              sumProf += float(thisAmt)
49              profList.append(tempList)
50          elif category == 'OTHER PUBLISHING EXPENSES':
51              sumOther += float(thisAmt)
52              otherList.append(tempList)
```

4.7 Append to the Category Lists

The function **sumtotals**() in the *lab2.py* file also takes "tempList" as an argument. For each category, the **sumtotals**() function appends "tempList" to the corresponding category list.

- Line 46 appends the "tempList" to "advList" when the category is "ADVERTISING."

- Line 49 appends the "tempList" to "profList" when the category is "LEGAL & PROFESSIONAL."

In *lab2.py*, on lines 41-42, I use the "global" keyword with the list variables, so that I can update these variables within the **sumTotals**() function. On line 46, I use the **.append**() string function to add "tempList" to "**advList**."

```
                              lab2.py
38  def sumTotals(category, thisAmt, tempList):
39          global sumAdv, sumOther, sumProf, sumOffice
40          global sumSupplies, sumMisc, sumAssets
```

```
41          global advList, otherList, profList, miscList
42          global officeList, assetsList, suppliesList
43
44          if category == 'ADVERTISING':
45              sumAdv += float(thisAmt)
46              advList.append(tempList)
47          elif category == 'LEGAL & PROFESSIONAL':
48              sumProf += float(thisAmt)
49              profList.append(tempList)
```

Each of these catgory lists contains lists of data from "filenames." For example, the "assetsList" has all business expenses for the category "Assets." In the diagram below, the display bar at the top of Variable Explorer tells you the type of the "assetsList" object, and the number of elements. The first (and only) element in **assetsList** is Index 0, the Type is "list," and the Size is "4" elements.

Figure 4.4   The assetsList

In the Python Console, if you type "**assetsList**" the Console displays the valueinside the assetsList. Notice there is one list in the "**assetsList**," and there are several nested lists inside of the "**otherList**." The "value" begins with two opening brackets and ends with two closing brackets, indicating these are list(s) inside of a list.

```
In [1]: assetsList
Out[1]: [['09/16/22', 'Apple Store Series 6 watch, '31.44', 'ASSETS']]
```

```
In [1]: otherList
Out[1]: [['04/14/20', 'Coreldraw', '12.90', 'OTHER PUBLISHING EXPENSES'],
        ['05/05/20', 'research -Book', '9.99', 'OTHER PUBLISHING EXPENSES'],
        ['06/26/20', 'Book Proof', '27.61', 'OTHER PUBLISHING EXPENSES']]
```

In Variable Explorer, if you double click on the element, a pop-up window opens with details about the four string elements inside that list element [0].

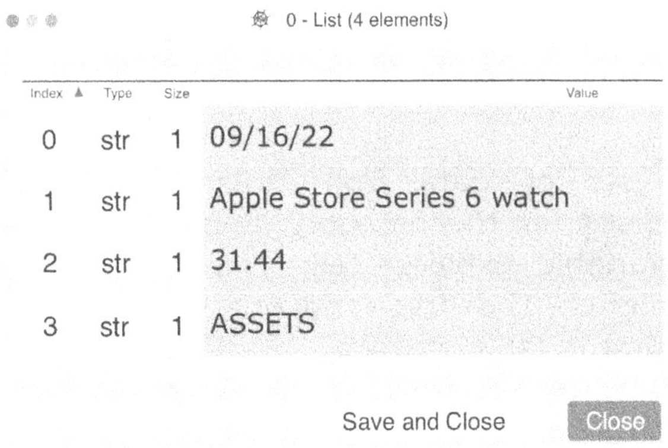
0 - List (4 elements)
Index Type Size Value
0 str 1 09/16/22
1 str 1 Apple Store Series 6 watch
2 str 1 31.44
3 str 1 ASSETS
Save and Close
Close

Figure 4.5 The four strings inside Element "0" inside the assetsList

5. Output to Excel

In this Chapter, we discuss

Preview Worksheet
Write Sum Totals to Worksheet
Create Category Worksheets
categoryWorksheet() Logic
Format Excel File
Save Excel File (with Date/timestamp)
Final Verification

Now that I have all my data, there are a few tasks to finalize my Excel workbook.

- Add sum totals to the top of the first worksheet, "Business_Expenses," followed on line 11 with all business expenses.

- Create seven "category" worksheets.

- Add Headings and format the workbook.

- Create the output filename.

5.1 Preview Worksheet

At this point, the "Business_Expenses" worksheet has data beginning on row 11, as shown below. There is a separate row of data for each filename. In the next topic, we'll add sum totals to rows 1-7. Later in this Chapter, we'll add headings to row 10 when we format the file.

	A	B	C	D
1				
2				
3				
4				
5				
6				
7				
8				
9				
10				
11	01/02/20	272.26	AMZ Advertising	ADVERTISING
12	01/07/20	39.00	training	OTHER MISC EXPENSES
13	01/08/20	450.00	Professional services CPA	LEGAL & PROFESSIONAL

Business_Expenses

In Chapter 3, we looked at line 77 in the *lab2.py* file, where the **row_out** variable is assigned to "11." The program begins writing data to row eleven of the "Business_Expenses" worksheet.

lab2.py Line	Column	Value
120	A	Date
121	B	Amount
122	C	Description
131	D	Category

lab2.py
120	ws.cell(row_out, 1).value = thisDate
121	ws.cell(row_out, 2).value = float(thisAmt)
122	ws.cell(row_out, 3).value = thisDesc

After I write category data to the fourth column on line 131, I increment the "row_out" counter on line 132 of the *lab2.py* file. As the loop continues through the filenames, I write data to row twelve and so on until there are worksheet rows for all the filenames.

lab2.py
127	if not thisCategory:
128	print("Couldn't find category for:", thisFileName)
129	else:
130	sumTotals(thisCategory, thisAmt, tempList)
131	ws.cell(row_out, 4).value = thisCategory
132	row_out += 1

5.2 Write Sum Totals to Worksheet

Line 132 of the *lab2.py* file calls the **writeSumTotalsToFile**() function. The function takes a worksheet object "ws," which is the "Business_Expenses" worksheet in the "Business_Expenses.xlsx" workbook, and seven float variables.

lab2.py
140	ws = writeSumTotalsToFile(ws, sumAdv, sumProf, sumOther, sumOffice,
141	sumAssets, sumSupplies, sumMisc)

Variable Explorer shows the seven float values.

Name	Type	Size	Value
sumAdv	float	1	272.26
sumAssets	float	1	31.44
sumMisc	float	1	50.4
sumOffice	float	1	31.31
sumOther	float	1	50.5
sumProf	float	1	450.0
sumSupplies	float	1	37.45

The writeSumTotalsToFile() Function

The function definition for **writeSumTotalsToFile**() begins on lines 21 to 22 of the *writeSumTotalsToFile.py* file. The expression is split over two lines.

> Python implements *implicit line joining*. Expressions in parentheses, square brackets, or curly braces can be split over more than one physical line without using backslashes.

Lines 24 to 30 call the **writeData**() helper function for each of the seven categories and lists. Finally, on line 32, I return the "ws" worksheet object to the calling expression on line 140 in the *lab2.py* file. Basically, I pass these four arguments to the **writeData**() function.

- ws - the worksheet object

- name (like "Advertising")

- the row number

- the sum total variable, (like sumAdv)

```
                        writeSumTotalsToFile.py
21   def writeSumTotalsToFile(ws, sumAdv, sumProf, sumOther, sumOffice,
22                          sumAssets, sumSupplies, sumMisc):
23
24       writeData(ws, 'Advertising', 1, sumAdv)
25       writeData(ws, 'Professional', 2, sumProf)
26       writeData(ws, 'Other', 3, sumOther)
27       writeData(ws, 'Office Expense', 4, sumOffice)
```

28	writeData(ws, 'Assets', 5, sumAssets)
29	writeData(ws, 'Supplies', 6, sumSupplies)
30	writeData(ws, 'Miscellaneous', 7, sumMisc)
31	
32	return ws

The writeData() Function

The helper **writeData**() function definition is on lines 9 to 18. There are comments on lines 10-12 that are not shown here. The **writeData**() function takes four arguments, as shown below.

- worksheet object (Business_Expenses)

- name (of the linked worksheet)

- row

- sum total

```
                          writeSumTotalsToFile.py
9    def writeData(ws, name, row, theSum):

10

13       theCell = '!A2'
14       file = "Business_Expenses.xlsx#'"
15       ws.cell(row, 3).value = name
16       ws.cell(row, 2).value = float(round(theSum, 2))
17       theLink = file + name + "'" + theCell
18       ws.cell(row, 2).hyperlink = theLink
```

Line 15 adds the "name" to Column C. For example, C3 is "Other." I also use the "name" variable when I create the hyperlink on line 17.

Line 16 adds "theSum" variable as a float in Column B. In the next example, cell B4 is "31.31," and the type is a float. Although I format the cell with the **.number_format**() method later in this chapter, I like to change the type to a float before I write data to the worksheet "ws" object so I can work with the data as numbers later in the Excel worksheet.

	A	B	C	D
1		272.26	Advertising	
2		450.00	Professional	
3		50.50	Other	
4		31.31	Office Expense	
5		31.44	Assets	
6		37.45	Supplies	
7		50.40	Misc	
Business_Expenses				

Line 18 creates a hyperlink from the "sum total" cell 'B3' on the <u>Business Expenses</u> worksheet to the corresponding 'A2' cell in the category worksheet.

	A		B
1	**Date**	**Description**	**Amount**
2	04/14/20	Coreldraw	12.90
3	05/05/20	research -Book	9.99
4	06/26/20	Book Proof	27.61
Other			

The hyperlink is from the current row in Column B of the "Business_Expenses" worksheet to the "A2" cell in the category worksheet. For example, the "Business_Expenses" cell "B3" links to cell "A2" in the "Other" worksheet. Note on line 14 the filename is hardcoded to "Business_Expenses.xlsx," so if I rename the Excel file, the links stop working. The final "B3" hyperlink is shown below.

Business_Expenses.xlsx#'Other'!A2

5.3 Create Category Worksheets

Before I call the **categoryWorksheets**() function in the *lab2.py* file, I sort all the individual category worksheets on lines 144-150. The first element in the "otherList" is a date, so in effect, I'm sorting by the date.

```
In [1]: otherList
Out[1]: [['04/14/20', 'Coreldraw', '12.90', 'OTHER PUBLISHING EXPENSES'],
        ['05/05/20', 'research -Book', '9.99', 'OTHER PUBLISHING EXPENSES'],
        ['06/26/20', 'Book Proof', '27.61', 'OTHER PUBLISHING EXPENSES']]
```

On lines 151-152, I call the **categoryWorksheets**() function and pass the workbook and the seven category lists as arguments. The expression begins on line 151 and ends on line 152.

> Python implements *implicit line joining*. Expressions in parentheses, square brackets, or curly braces can be split over more than one physical line without using backslashes.

lab2.py

```
144  advList.sort()
145  otherList.sort()
146  profList.sort()
147  officeList.sort()
148  assetsList.sort()
149  suppliesList.sort()
150  miscList.sort()
151  wb = categoryWorksheets(wb, advList, otherList, profList, officeList,
152      assetsList, suppliesList, miscList)
```

Category Data and Output

Before we dig into the code in the **categoryWorksheets**() function, I will walk through how the data is laid out and explain how to use "indexing" to access data in Python lists.

Each of these category lists contains embedded lists of the values gathered from the "filenames." In the Console, type **assetsList**. The Console displays the data shown below. There are two opening brackets and two closing brackets, indicating this is a list embedded in a list.

```
In [1]: assetsList
Out[1]: [['09/16/22', 'Apple Store Series 6 watch, '31.44', 'ASSETS']]
```

Now let's use indexing to only look at the first element, or list, in the "assetsList." Python starts counting at zero, so the first element is **assetsList[0]**. In the Console, type **assetsList[0]**. The Console displays the data shown below. Now there is only one set of opening and closing square brackets.

```
In [2]: assetsList[0]
Out[2]: ['09/16/22', 'Apple Store Series 6 watch, '31.44', 'ASSETS']
```

In the Console, experiment with different indexing to see any of the four string values inside the list. Because these values are strings, they are enclosed in parentheses.

```
In [3]: assetsList[0][0]
Out[3]: '09/16/22'
```

```
In [4]: assetsList[0][2]
Out[4]: '31.44'
```

In Variable Explorer, open the "assetsList" and double-click on the first element. A pop-up window opens displaying four "string" elements, as shown in the next diagram.

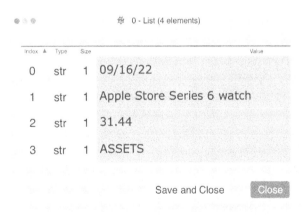

Figure 5.1   The element "0" list inside the assetsList, with 4 elements

These four string values represent data from the filename.

- Date

- Description

- Amount

- Category

Because Python begins counting at zero, the first element is **assetsList[0]**, which is a list in our example. A "list" is a sequence object with an internal data structure that is iterable. Python uses indexing to support efficient element access of iterable objects. The next table shows the indexing for elements in assetsList[**0**]. Notice each example begins with **assetsList[0]**, indicating the first element in "assetsList."

First list in assetsList	Four Elements Inside assetsList[0]
assetsList[**0**][0]	09/16/22
assetsList[**0**][1]	Apple Store Series 6 watch
assetsList[**0**][2]	31.44
assetsList[**0**][3]	ASSETS

- The first element, in the first list in assetsList, is assetsList[**0**][0] with a value of 09/16/22.

- The third element, in the first list in assetsList, is assetsList[**0**][2], with a value of 31.44.

The **categoryWorksheets**() function writes the data from the seven lists to seven worksheets. For example, the **miscList** data is written to the "Miscellaneous" worksheet, as shown below. The date, amount, and description are in columns A, B, and C, respectively.

	A		B
1	**Date**	**Description**	**Amount**
2	01/07/20	training	39.00
3	10/04/20	Editing	11.40
	Miscellaneous		

5.4 categoryWorksheets() Logic

Now that you've seen the finished product let's go back to the *categoryWorksheets.py* file and review the code. There are three tasks in this script, repeated for each category worksheet and list. The **categoryWorksheets**() function definition begins on line 20 and takes eight arguments.

- Create a worksheet.

- Write data from the list to the worksheet with the **list_2_worksheet**() function.

- Format the category worksheet

```
                              categoryWorksheets.py
17   from formatExcelFile import formatCategoryWs
18
19
20   def categoryWorksheets(wb, advList, otherList, profList, officeList,
21                          assetsList, suppliesList, miscList):
22       wsAdv = wb.create_sheet('Advertising')
23       wsOther = wb.create_sheet('Other')
24       wsProf = wb.create_sheet('Professional')
25       wsOffice = wb.create_sheet('Office Supplies')
26       wsAssets = wb.create_sheet('Assets')
27       wsSupplies = wb.create_sheet('Supplies')
28       wsMisc = wb.create_sheet('Miscellaneous')
29
30       list_2_worksheet(advList, wsAdv)
31       list_2_worksheet(otherList, wsOther)
32       list_2_worksheet(profList, wsProf)
33       list_2_worksheet(officeList, wsOffice)
34       list_2_worksheet(assetsList, wsAssets)
35       list_2_worksheet(suppliesList, wsSupplies)
36       list_2_worksheet(miscList, wsMisc)
37
38       wsAdv = formatCategoryWs(wsAdv, advList)
39       wsOther = formatCategoryWs(wsOther, otherList)
40       wsProf = formatCategoryWs(wsProf, profList)
41       wsAssets = formatCategoryWs(wsAssets, assetsList)
42       wsOffice = formatCategoryWs(wsOffice, officeList)
43       wsSupplies = formatCategoryWs(wsSupplies, suppliesList)
44       wsMisc = formatCategoryWs(wsMisc, miscList)
45       return wb
46
47
48   def list_2_worksheet(theList, ws):
49       items = len(theList)
50       outRow = 2
```

```
51          for item in range(items):
52              for col in range(3):
53                  ws.cell(row=outRow, column=col + 1).value = theList[item][col]
54              outRow += 1
```

Import the Module

In the *categoryWorksheets.py* file, line 17 imports a module from the "*formatExcelFile.py*" file. We'll look at this function in detail later in this Chapter.

```
                            categoryWorksheets.py
17   from formatExcelFile import formatCategoryWs
```

Create Seven Category Worksheets.

Lines 22-28 call the **.create_sheet**() method from the **openpyxl** library to create seven worksheets for the "wb" workbook object.

```
                            categoryWorksheets.py
20   def categoryWorksheets(wb, advList, otherList, profList, officeList,
21                   assetsList, suppliesList, miscList):
22       wsAdv = wb.create_sheet('Advertising')
23       wsOther = wb.create_sheet('Other')
24       wsProf = wb.create_sheet('Professional')
25       wsOffice = wb.create_sheet('Office Supplies')
26       wsAssets = wb.create_sheet('Assets')
27       wsSupplies = wb.create_sheet('Supplies')
28       wsMisc = wb.create_sheet('Miscellaneous')
```

Add data to Worksheets

On lines 30-36, I call the **list_2_worksheet**() function for each category list. The **list_2_worksheet**() function definition is also part of the *categoryWorkshets.py* file; and takes two arguments, a list, and a worksheet. For the **miscList** and **wsMisc** worksheet, the function call is on line 36, as shown below.

```
list_2_worksheet(miscList, wsMisc)
```

The **list_2_worksheet**() function is defined from lines 48-54.

```
categoryWorksheets.py
30    list_2_worksheet(advList, wsAdv)
31    list_2_worksheet(otherList, wsOther)
32    list_2_worksheet(profList, wsProf)
33    list_2_worksheet(officeList, wsOffice)
34    list_2_worksheet(assetsList, wsAssets)
35    list_2_worksheet(suppliesList, wsSupplies)
36    list_2_worksheet(miscList, wsMisc)
```

Line 49 gets the length of "theList" and assigns it to the "**items**" variable. The **len**() function returns the number of elements in "theList." Line 50 assigns the "outRow" variable to "2" because I want to begin writing to row two in the category worksheet.

	A		B
		Business_Expenses.xlsx	
1	**Date**	**Description**	**Amount**
2	01/02/20	AMZ Advertising	272.26
		Advertising	

The **range**() function on line 51 takes a start and stop argument. This expression is the first control statement or "loop." Since only one argument is provided, the **range**() function uses the default "0" as the start argument and uses the "**items**" variable as the stop argument. In effect, the control loop on line 51 iterates over all **items** in "theList."

```
categoryWorksheets.py
48    def list_2_worksheet(theList, ws):
49        items = len(theList)
50        outRow = 2
51        for item in range(items):
52            for col in range(3):
53                ws.cell(row=outRow, column=col + 1).value = theList[item][col]
54            outRow += 1
```

There is a second control statement on line 52 for the columns. The **range**() function on line 52 assigns the "**col**" variable to 0-1-2, and iterates over columns 0-1-2, or A-B-C. This control statement for the columns begins on line 52 and ends on line 53. Line 53 uses indexing to retrieve values from the "theList," and writes each value to the corresponding column.

The **miscList** shown below has two lists.

Two lists in miscList	Elements Inside miscList[0] and miscList[1]
miscList[0][0]	01/07/20
miscList[0][1]	training
miscList[0][2]	39.00
miscList[0][3]	OTHER MISC EXPENSES
miscList[1][0]	10/04/20
miscList[1][1]	Editing
miscList[1][2]	11.40
miscList[1][3]	OTHER MISC EXPENSES

This "column loop" is inside the first control statement (lines 51 to line 54,) which iterates over each "**item**" in the list. In effect, as I loop through each **item** in the list, I also loop through columns and write the columns A, B, and C for that **item**.

```
ws.cell(row=outRow, column=col + 1).value = theList[item][col]
```

Format the Category Worksheets

In the *categoryWorksheets.py* file, lines 38-44 call the **formatCategoryWs**() function seven times for each category worksheet. The seven worksheets are shown below.

List	Worksheet Name
advList	Advertising
profList	Professional
otherList	Other
officeList	Office Supplies
assetsList	Assets
suppliesList	Supplies
miscList	Miscellaneous

categoryWorksheets.py

```
38      wsAdv = formatCategoryWs(wsAdv, advList)

39      wsOther = formatCategoryWs(wsOther, otherList)

40      wsProf = formatCategoryWs(wsProf, profList)

41      wsAssets = formatCategoryWs(wsAssets, assetsList)

42      wsOffice = formatCategoryWs(wsOffice, officeList)

43      wsSupplies = formatCategoryWs(wsSupplies, suppliesList)

44      wsMisc = formatCategoryWs(wsMisc, miscList)

45      return wb
```

The **formatCategoryWs**() function sets the column width, adds headings, and formats the font for the category worksheets. All the category worksheets have the same basic settings.

The function definition for **formatCategoryWs**() begins on line 40 in the *formatExcelFile.py* file. Lines 41 and 42 add a heading. Line 43 freezes the row above and to the left of "E2."

In the *categoryWorksheets.py* file, line 43 turns on filtering from cell "A1" to the last row in column C. The last row value is from the **.max_row** method of the "ws" worksheet object. Lines 45-47 set the column width. Line 48 calls the **formatCommon**() function, which we'll look at in the next topic.

Finally, line 49 of the *formatExcelFile.py* in the formatCateegoryWs function returns the "ws" workstation object to the calling expression on line 17 in the **formatExcel File**() function, or line 48 in the **formatCategoryWs**() function.

	formatExcelFile.py
40	def formatCategoryWs(ws):
41	ws.cell(1, 3).value = "Amount"
42	ws.cell(1, 2).value = "Description"
43	ws.freeze_panes = 'E2'
44	ws.auto_filter.ref = "A1:C" + str(ws.max_row)
45	ws.column_dimensions['A'].width = 13
46	ws.column_dimensions['B'].width = 25
47	ws.column_dimensions['C'].width = 30
48	ws = formatCommon(ws, 1)
49	return ws

Return Statement

In the *categoryWorksheets.py* file, line 45, I return the "wb" workbook object to the calling script, *lab2.py*.

5.5 Format Excel File

The **formatExcelFile**() function is called on line 154 and formats the first worksheet in the file, "Business_Expenses."

	lab2.py
153	
154	ws = formatExcelFile(ws)
155	
156	wb.save(getFilename())
157	wb.save('Business_Expenses.xlsx')

The **formatExcelFile**() function adds the headings on row 10 in the "Business_Expenses" worksheet and sets some other format settings.

	A	B	C	D
1		272.26	Advertising	
2		450.00	Professional	
3		50.50	Other	
4		31.31	Office Expense	
5		31.44	Assets	
6		37.45	Supplies	
7		50.40	Misc	
8				
9				
10	**Date**	**Amount**	**Description**	**Category**
11	01/02/20	272.26	AMZ Advertising	ADVERTISING
12	01/07/20	39.00	training	OTHER MISC EXPENSES
13	01/08/20	450.00	Professional services CPA	LEGAL & PROFESSIONAL
			Business_Expenses	

The first few lines of the *formatExcelFile.py* file assign values for the common variables I use in several formatting functions. Line 2 imports "Font" and "Alignment" from the "openpyxl.styles" library. These are some of the basic formatting options I used.

- wra text

- horizontal & vertical alignment

- font: name, bold, size

- column width

- headings

- format cell-number: 0.00 (float)

- format cell-number: date

- print gridlines

- row height

- freeze panes

- auto-filter

	formatExcelFile.py
2	from openpyxl.styles import Font, Alignment
3	alignment1 = Alignment(wrapText=True,
4	horizontal='left',
5	vertical='center')
6	alignment2 = Alignment(horizontal='center',
7	vertical='center')
8	ft = Font(name='Tahoma', bold=True, size="11")
9	

The function definition for **formatExcelFile**() begins on line 11 of the *formatExcelFile.py* file. The **formatExcelFile**() function takes a worksheet "ws" object as the only argument.

	formatExcelFile.py
11	def formatExcelFile(ws):
12	ws.column_dimensions['B'].width = 13
13	ws.column_dimensions['C'].width = 25
14	ws.column_dimensions['D'].width = 30
15	ws.cell(10, 2).value = "Amount"
16	ws.cell(10, 3).value = "Description"
17	ws = formatCommon(ws, 10)
18	ws.cell(10, 4).value = "Category"
19	for row in range(1, ws.max_row + 1):
20	ws.cell(row, 2).number_format = "0.00"
21	return ws

On lines 12-14, I set the column width. On lines 15, 16, and 18, I add headings. On line 17, I call the helper function **formatCommon**(), which I'll discuss in the next topic. Lines 19-20 are a control statement "for loop" that iterates through all rows in the "ws" worksheet, setting the cell number format for column 2. Finally, on line 21, the function returns the "ws" worksheet object.

Line 24 is the function definition for the helper function **formatCommon**(). Line 25 adds a heading to column 1. Line 26 turns on gridlines. Line 27 changes the cell number format to "0.00" or a float with two decimals. Lines 28-36 are a "for loop" that iterates through all rows in the "ws" worksheet. Lines 28 and 29 set the bold font for the headings.

Within the row "for loop" is a nested loop on lines 34 to 36 that iterates over columns 1-4 changing the alignment and font. Earlier on lines 3-8, I set the values for alignment and font. Line 37 returns the "ws" worksheet object to the calling function or row 17 within the **formatExcelFile**() function.

formatExcelFile.py

```
24   def formatCommon(ws, row):
25       ws.cell(row, 1).value = "Date"
26       ws.print_options.gridLines = True
27       ws.cell(row, 2).number_format = "0.00"
28       for col in range(1, 5):
29           ws.cell(row, col).font = ft
30       for row in range(1, ws.max_row + 1):
31           ws.row_dimensions[row].height = 18
32           ws.cell(row, 1).number_format = "DD MM YY"
33           ws.cell(row, 1).alignment = alignment2
34           for col in range(1, 5):
35               ws.cell(row, col).alignment = alignment1
36               ws.cell(row, col).font = ft
37       return ws
```

5.6 Save File

To demonstrate adding a timestamp to your filename, I import the **getFilename**() function on line 14. Essentially **getFilename**() just creates a filename with a path for the output file. On line 156, I save the workbook object "wb" and pass it the filename returned by **getFilename**(). The wb.**save()** method expects the filename as a string object. On line 157, I save the "wb" again with a different filename.

getFilename.py

```
14   def getFilename():
15       from datetime import datetime
16       import os
17
18       mypath = os.environ['HOME']
19       mypath += '/BOOK_AUTHORING/Python_Lab2/CODE_for_Lab2/results/'
20       d1 = datetime.strftime(datetime.now(), '%m%d%Y  %H_%M_%p')
21       return mypath + d1 + ' Business Expenses.xlsx'
```

In the *getFilename.py* file, line 15 imports the "datetime" library and **.datetime**. Line 16 imports the "os" library, and line 18 uses the "os" library method **.environ** to get my computer's **home** directory.

Line 20 retrieves the date and time with the **.now**() function from the "datetime" library. Line 20 also uses the **.strftime**() function to format the value as a string object.

The **getFilename**() function returns a string object on line 21, as shown below. The wb.**save**() method expects a filename with path as a string parameter

> /BOOK_AUTHORING/Python_Lab2/CODE_for_Lab2/results/ 05292021   07_42_AM Business Expenses.xlsx

To demonstrate using the **.save** method, on line 157 in the *lab2.py* file, I save the "wb" object again with a different filename. Essentially I create two identical workbooks with different names.

5.7 Final Verification

As a check to make sure I have a categorized receipt for every "filename," I compare the length of "files" to the rows on the "ws" worksheet. Line 164 prints a message with the data.

lab2.py
160 total_ReceiptsCategorized = ws.max_row - 9
161 total_Files = len(files)
162 msg1 = "There are " + str(total_Files) + " files and"
163 msg2 = str(total_ReceiptsCategorized) + " categorized receipts."
164 print(msg1, msg2)

6. Python Basics

In this Chapter, we discuss

Python Syntax

Objects

Immutable Objects

Variables

Expressions

Types of Data

Numbers

Data Structures

Strings

Lists

Methods for Lists

Dictionary

Range

Indexes

Slicing

Operators

Identifiers

Compound Statements

Indented Code (a Suite)

Functions & Methods

Classes

Modules & Libraries

Attributes

Scope, Namespace & Memory

In this Chapter, we'll take a brief look at a few basic Python concepts. This chapter is by no means a complete Python language guide; instead, think of it as an abbreviated part of the Python language documentation. I need this small subset of information to demonstrate how you will refer back to the Python documentation.

6.1   Python Syntax

The Spyder Integrated Development Environment (IDE) includes an **Editor** that warns you when you have a syntax error in your script. A yellow triangle on the left side of the Editor pane next to the line number indicates an error. Next, we'll look at a few common causes of syntax errors. The python.org site has the **PEP** documents, or Python Enhancement Proposals.

- Valid characters for variable names or identifiers vary between Python 2.x and Python 3.x. Python 3 added support for Unicode characters in PEP 3131 to accommodate programmers who are unfamiliar with the English language. To avoid errors, I adhere to these guidelines.

  - Identifiers begin with a letter.

  - Numbers are allowed in object names, except as the first character. Object names are also known as identifiers.

  - In Python 2.x, the only special character allowed in an identifier name is an underscore. Instead of spaces in identifier names, try an underscore. Illegal spaces or characters like $, #, and @ will cause a syntax error.

- The PEP 8 Style Guide suggests lowercase characters for identifier names and functions. A PEP is a design document providing information to the Python community. Classes begin with an uppercase letter. For example, variables and list names are lowercase.

- Python is case sensitive. There is a difference between "myString" and "mystring." The Python Interpreter displays a NameError when there is a misspelled identifier.

- When defining a function or control statement, the line should always end with a colon.

- Text to the right of the # hash character is a comment. You can add comments anywhere in the line.

- A data structure name should be plural, and items in the data set should be singular. For example, a **List** named "vacations" with List items: vacation[0], vacation[1], etc.

- Do not use reserved <u>keywords</u> as <u>identifiers</u>. A missing keyword in a function call causes a SyntaxError. Functions also have <u>keyword arguments</u>.

- An empty Suite <u>(indented</u> block of code) is illegal. See "<u>Indented Code (Suite)</u>" later in this Chapter for more information.

Python has reserved **keywords** like "global" or "try." When you use a keyword as a variable name, it causes a syntax error. To see keywords, in the Console type **help("keywords")**.

Referencing Object Values

To begin you may ask, "How do I get the value inside a variable." At any time, you can type the object name in the Console, and the Python Interpreter will display the value at that moment. Here my variable "mystr" has a value of "apple."

In [**1**]: mystr

Out[1]: apple

Variables in Imported Modules

To reference a class attribute or a variable inside another <u>module</u>, use <u>dotted notation</u>. In this script, I <u>import</u> a module "mymodule2" that has the variable "mystr2." The expression **module2.mystr2** returns the value of **mystr2**.

```
1    import mymodule2
2    print(mymodule2.mystr2)
```

6.2 Objects

The building blocks of Python are objects. Objects have an identity, type, and value and are Python's abstraction for data.

- Data with state

- Defined behavior (methods)

State refers to the properties of an object, the attributes or value of the object. The object's behavior is how the Python Interpreter interacts with that type of object.

The "identifier" or "identity" of the object is the "name" of the object. With the library "**openpyxl**," you assign **objects** to both the workbook and worksheet, and then you use those **objects** with **methods** to read or update values (the data). In this example "wb2" is the name of the workbook. There is also a unique "identifier" associated with the object "wb2." In the next topic we'll look at a variable "bfr" and bfr's identifier.

```
1    from openpyxl import load_workbook
2    wb2 = load_workbook('myfile.xlsx', data_only = True)
3    ws2 = wb2["ExportedData"]
```

6.3 Immutable Objects

In Python, strings, numbers, and "tuple" types are immutable, meaning the values are fixed and can't change. While you can **not** change existing strings, numbers (integers or floats) or tuples, you can create new objects with changed data to replace objects.

If you're new to programming, this concept may seem strange. Take the case of a Python object of the type "**int**." The code statement **bfr = bfr + 1** seems to change the value of **bfr**. In reality, this statement creates a new object. The new object has a new identifier and a different location in memory. To see this in action, run this code in the **Console** to see the identifiers for the **bfr** objects.

```
In [1]: bfr = 'Hello'
In [2]: print(id(bfr))
Out [2]: 12345678

In [3]: bfr = bfr + 1
In [4]: print(id(bfr))
Out [4]: 9876543210
```

The comparison operator "is" returns "True" when two variables point to the same object in memory, as shown later in the topic "Operators."

Immutable objects are quicker to access and hashable, and this improves code performance. Another advantage of immutable objects is understandability, and knowing the object will never change.

The Python definition of "hashable" is an object that "has a hash value which never changes during its lifetime (it needs a __hash__() method), and can be compared to other objects (it needs an __eq__() method)." We'll look at these special methods at the end of this chapter.

__hash__()

__eq__()

6.4 Variables

In Python, a variable name refers to an object. An object is a place in memory that has a **value** such as a letter or number. An **assignment statement** or "binding" creates a variable and binds or associates the name with an object. The object is a place in memory. *You must have an equal number of variables and values on the left and right side of the assignment statement.*

Python is case sensitive, and mixing case can cause a **NameError**. Special characters like $, #, and @ are not allowed for variable names and cause an error. The left side of an assignment statement must be a variable name, and the right side is a value. The assignment operator is the equals = sign.

mynumber = 2000000

The Python style guide suggests that variable names begin with a letter.

Indirection is using a name to refer to an object. When you add "mynumber" to a list named "mylist," there are two levels of indirection. When a program runs, the **variable** might be assigned a different value; meaning the variable name might be assigned to a different object in memory, or the object itself might be updated.

Global Variables

When you have a variable with a different value than you expected, it may be due to scope. When you run the program, the Python Interpreter creates variables and adds them to the "global scope" or the first memory "stack." While the program execution remains in this suite of code, the objects are also in the "local scope." In Python, you can read, but not change, the value of a global variable at any point in your program or from within functions, as long as everything is within the **same *.py file**.

Each time the code moves into a "function," a new "local" scope is created. Within the local scope of a function, you can't **change** the values of objects in the outer global scope or enclosing scopes. *At any time, you can only change values within the local scope.* When you create objects inside a function or method, those objects or variables are typically not available outside the scope of that function. To change a global variable within a function, use the keyword "global" to make the global variable part of the "local" scope.

We look at scope in detail at the end of this chapter in the topic, "Scope, Namespace, and Memory."

A word of warning about global variables, they are dangerous! It's easy to lose track of which function is updating a global variable. To avoid global variables, try a recursive function and pass the data through an optional function parameter.

> In a bit, we'll look at using a function argument with a default value as another way to implement the concept of a "global variable." There is an example of this process in the "Function" topic "optional arguments" later in this chapter, as well as the topic recursive functions.

In the next diagram, the program has "var1" in the main body of the program (lines 5-7) and "var2" (on line 2) within myfunction().

To explore global variables, run this code in debug mode and step through the code, running one line at a time.

1. The Python Interpreter evaluates the **function definition** on line 1 and quickly moves to line 5. If myfunction() had <u>optional arguments</u> with default values, they are assigned using the "scope" that exists at line 1 (the global scope.)

    If there had been an error within the **function definition**, the interpreter would stop and raise the error.

2. The Python Interpreter then runs line 6.

3. If you choose to "**step into**" myfunction() on line 6, the code moves up to line 1.

4. Next, the code moves inside the function, to lines 2 and 3. At this point, you'll see Variable Explorer displays both var1 and var2.

5. The program then moves back to line 7. At this point, var2 disappears from Variable Explorer, and that "scope" is gone.

```
1   def myfunction():
2         var2 = 4
3         print(var2)
4
5   var1 = 7
6   myfunction()
7   print(var1)
```

In the next block of code, let's explore using "var1" inside of "myfunction." This code runs as expected and prints "var1" on line 2 because I'm not trying to change the value of var1.

```
1   def myfunction():
2         print(var1)
3         var2 = 4
4         print(var2)
5
6
7   var1 = 7
```

```
8  myfunction()
9  print(var1)
```

However, it's a different story if I attempt to change "var1" within myfunction(). This next code causes an error and the **Console** displays the UnboundLocalError shown below. The **UnboundLocalError** is raised because "var1" does not exist within the local scope of "myfunction()."

"UnboundLocalError" local variable 'var1' referenced before assignment.

```
1  def myfunction():
2      print(var1)
3      var2 = 4
4      var1 = 9
5
6
7  var1 = 7
8  myfunction()
9  print(var1)
```

To prevent the UnboundLocalError use the keyword "global" to declare "var1" a global variable on line 2 inside myfunction(). Notice in the next example there is no "**assignment**" value on line 2. When line 3 prints "var1," it has a value of "7" from the assignment statement for "var1" on line 7 in the main program. Line 5 assigns "9" to the global variable "var1" within the local scope of myfunction(). When line 9 prints "var1," the value is now 9.

You can read more about scope and namespace at the end of this chapter.

```
1   def myfunction():
2       global var1
3       print(var1)
4       var2 = 4
5       var1 = 9
6
7
8   var1 = 7
9   myfunction()
10  print(var1)
```

Unpacking

When you **unpack** a tuple or list you assign individual elements to new variables. We'll look at unpacking later in this chapter in the topic, "Functions, Unpacking Operator. In the next example, **mytuple** has four elements. On the second line, I unpack the four tuple elements and assign them to four variables.

```
In [1]: mytuple = (1, 2, 3, 4)
In [2]: myvar1, myvar2, myvar3, myvar4 = mytuple
```

Ignore or Throw Away Variables

Sometimes you'll see code where the underscore character is used when a programmer wants to ignore an element in a tuple or list. These are often called "throw away" variables. In the second statement below, the "2" element is assigned to the underscore _. In the third statement I use the variable "dummy" as a "throw away" variable, which may provide more clarity.

```
a, b, c, d = (1, 2, 3, 4)
a, _, c, d = (1, 2, 3, 4)
a, dummy, c, d = (1, 2, 3, 4)
```

The PEP 3132 "Extended Iterable Unpacking" specifies a "catch-all" name which is assigned to a list of all items not assigned to a "regular" name.

```
1    a, *b = (1, 2, 3, 4)
```

The result is "a" = 1 and "b" is a tuple: (2, 3, 4).

6.5   **Expressions**

An expression is a piece of syntax that evaluates to some value. The actions that a program takes are referred to as "expressions" or statements. A simple statement is comprised in a single logical line. A compound statement contains groups of other statements; for example: for, with, or while. Objects, literals, names, function calls and operators are combined to form expressions.

```
<object><operator><object>

myvar = 7
```

We'll look at <u>comparison operators,</u> compound control statements, and <u>loops</u> later in this Chapter.

Comments

Code <u>comments</u> begin with the hash # symbol.

Joining Lines

Python uses <u>explicit line joining</u>. Expressions that span more than one physical line are joined into logical lines with a backslash.

```
print('the swift fox jumped over the \
lazy dog and then ran into the briar patch.'
```

Python also implements <u>implicit line joining</u>. Expressions in parentheses, square brackets, or curly braces can be split over more than one physical line without using backslashes.

Escape Sequence

Special characters in strings are identified with an "<u>escape sequence</u>" or backslash. For example, the line feed character is '**\n**' within a string. When you add the 'r' prefix the raw quotes tell the Python Interpreter to ignore the escape sequence so that the backslash is simply a backslash character.

```
r'c:\users'
```

In the previous example, if you omit the prefix '**r**,' a SyntaxError is raised.

SyntaxError: (unicode error) 'unicodeescape' codec can't decode bytes in position 2-3: truncated \uXXXX escape

Apostrophes in strings also use escape sequences, with a backslash as shown below.

mystr = `\"'

In the Editor, when you hover your mouse over a parenthesis, the paired parenthesis is highlighted in green. If a parentheses is missing, the starting parenthesis is highlighted in orange.

6.6   Types of Data

Python has several types of data. Numeric primitives such as "floats" and "ints" are scalar objects, in that there is no internal structure. A 'bool' and the "None" type are also primitive scalar objects. A string is a non-scalar primitive object, and you use an index to indicate the position within the string. Moving through items using an index is referred to as iteration.

Containers are non-scalar objects with internal structures. Examples of container objects are a list, tuple, dictionary, or range. A range was introduced with Python v3. We'll look at these data structures in-depth in later topics. For now, a few of the basic data types are shown in the next table.

Type	Description	Assignment	Value(s)
int	integer	my_var = 3	3
float	floating-point number	my_var = 3.85	3.85
bool	boolean (true/false)	my_var4 = False	False
NoneType	Function with no return value	myfunction()	None
str	string of characters	my_var2 = 'Hi'	Hi
tuple	any type of data - immutable	mytuple = ('Hi', 4)	Hi, 4
list	any type of data - mutable	mylist = [4, 9, 'hi']	4, 9, hi
range	integers - immutable	range(4, 9)	4, 5, 6, 7, 8

Table 6.1   Data Types

When my_var = 3, the statement **float(my_var+5)** returns **8.0**.

When my_var = 3, the statement **print(34//my_var)** returns **11**.

In the case of the statement **3 == 3**, the Python Interpreter returns "True."

Boolean Values

A <u>boolean value</u> is either "False" or "True" and behaves like the integers 0 and 1 respectively. Therefore, the statement "not 0" is True.

```
In [1]: not 0
Out[1]: True
```

The next example uses the "**modulo**" operator "**%**" that returns the remainder when dividing two numbers. This expression returns "0" indicating there is no remainder. In simple terms I am asking, "does x % 7 have a remainder?" and the answer is "no" or "0."

```
In [1]: x = 21
In [2]: x % 7
Out[2]: 0
```

When combined with the <u>boolean "not" operator</u> the expression is "True."I n this example I am asking, "is it true that x % 7 does not have a remainder?" and the answer is "yes that is True."

```
In [3]: x = 21
In [4]: not x % 7
Out[4]: True
```

What is the Data Type?

If you're unsure of an object's type, the **type()** function displays the type of data. The second statement below uses the "<u>isinstance()</u>" function that returns "True" when an object is the specified type. In this example, I am testing if the "mystr" is a "str" type. To see this in action, type the code in the Editor and click "run."

```
1    print(type(mystr))
2    print(isinstance(mystr, str))
```

Later in this chapter, we'll look at identifying types of objects in dictionaries in the topic, "<u>Find the Type of a Dictionary Element</u>."

Converting Data Types

When working with data, you may need to change or convert the data type. In other programming languages this is called casting. For example, during a calculation, you may want to convert between a **float** and an **int** to remove decimal places.

int(my_var)

str(my_var)

float(my_var)

bool(my_var)

Converting Floats to Ints

Notice in this example the value "45.9" is converted to "45."

```
1    myfloat = 45.9
2    int(myfloat)
```

The next statement rounds the float number up to the whole number "46."

```
1    myfloat = 45.9
2    round(myfloat, 0)
```

Converting Strings to Ints

When concatenating numeric values and strings, the statement str(**my_int**) converts the string to an integer. While I can't convert the string '1.25' into a whole number **int**, it is legal to first convert the string to a float, and then convert the float to an int.

NoneType or None

In Python, the absence of a value is called "None," which is capitalized. The type is "NoneType" and the value is "None." In other languages, this would be a null value. A function with no return statement returns the value "None." When working with external data sources, you may have to account for this type of value. An "if statement" that tests for a value of "None" is shown below.

```
1   if myvar is not None:
2       pass
```

To check if a string variable has a value you can use the syntax on line 2 in the example below. The variable "mystr1" is assigned to "None" on line 1, and "mystr2" is assigned to an empty string. In this example, I'm testing whether the variables have no value. Line 6 also evaluates to True and is equivalent to the logic on line 2.

```
1   mystr1, mystr2 = None, ''
2   if mystr1 is not None and mystr2 != '':
3       print('mystr1 and mystr2 have a value')
4   else:
5       print('mystr1 and mystr2 do not have a value')
6   if mystr1 and mystr2:
7       print('mystr1 and mystr2 have avalue')
8   else:
9       print('mystr1 and mystr2 do not have a value')
```

In this example, I could compare the type of "mystr" on line 2 to **type(None)**; however, the preferred expression is to use "isinstance," as shown on line 5. The expression on line 2 would return "**True**."

```
1   mystr = None
2   if type(mystr) is type(None):
3       print('the type of mystr is None')
4
5   print(isinstance(mystr, str))
```

6.7 Numbers

Floats and integer types represent numbers in Python and are scalar objects that have no internal data structure. When assigning integer values to variables, do not use commas. Python interprets 2,000,000 as three integers separated by commas.

mynumber = 2000000

In the previous example, I assign 2000000 to the integer variable "**mynumber**." For readability, in Python 3.6 and later, you can add underscores as a separator.

mynumber = 2_000_000

Floating Point Numbers

Non-integer numbers or floats are stored in computer memory as a binary representation of 0's and 1's. Calculations can introduce subtle differences where you may think both float values are 1.08, but the actual binary representation is slightly different.

The function **repr()** displays a printable representation of a float, and is useful in troubleshooting rounding errors.

> The "comparison" topic later in this chapter has details on comparing 'floating point' numbers.

NAN

A <u>NAN</u> is a special floating-point value that can't be converted. NAN stands for "not a number." The "math" function math.**isnan(x)** returns True if "x" isn't a number.

6.8   Data Structures

Python has several built-in compound data structures or sequence types for non-scalar objects. Non-scalar objects have an internal structure. A list, tuple, or range is a sequence type. A string is a **text sequence type**. Objects that contain references to other objects are "<u>containers</u>." These data structures have an ordered sequence of **elements** or items. That is not to say the items are arranged in a particular order, but rather that Python assigns a sequence of indexes to the items.

The **docs.python.org** site refers to containers or sequence objects as "<u>iterables</u>." Iterables are objects with a sequence of elements referenced by an index. You use an index to iterate through these containers to access the value of a particular element in the container.

- Lists
- Tuples
- Strings
- Range

We'll look at iterables later in this chapter in the topic, "Control Statements - Iterables."

While there are other data structures in Python, the last common one we'll look at in-depth is a dictionary. A dictionary is a "mapping type" of data. Later in this chapter we'll briefly look at set, zip, map, and filter data structures.

- Dictionary
- Set
- Zip
- Map
- Filter

Python uses the operations listed below for all of these data structures. Later in this chapter, we'll look at these common operations, and you'll see the syntax is the same regardless of whether you're working with a list, tuple, string, or dictionary. For example, the function len() tells you how many objects are in the data structure. In the case of a string, len() tells you how many characters are in the string. For a list, len() tells you how many elements are in the list.

- len()
- Comparison operators "in" and "not in"
- Control loops like "for"

A list, tuple, or string also uses these operations, which we'll look at in detail later in this chapter.

- Indexing
- Slicing

With the exception of a range, you can use concatenation and multiplication on data structures. For example, to concatenate two lists using the plus "+" symbol, use the expression **mylist1 + mylist2**.

- Concatenation
- Multiplication

Tuples also support concatenation, as shown below.

In [**1**]: mytuple = (1,'two', 3)

In [**2**]: mytuple
Out [**2**]: (1, 'two', 3)

In [**3**]: mytuple + ('H', 2, 'O')

In [**4**]: mytuple
Out [**4**]: (1,'two', 3, 'H', 2, 'O')

6.9   Strings

A **string** is a sequence of characters. These non-scalar objects have an internal data structure accessed through indexes. To assign a value to a string variable, use single quotation mark '' or double quotation "" marks, as shown below. When you add the 'r' prefix the raw quotes tell the Python Interpreter the backslash is a literal backslash character and not an escape sequence.

b = 'bookstore'

If you forget the closing apostrophe in your assignment statement, a SyntaxError is raised for "EOL while scanning string literal." A byte literal is prefixed with a 'b' or 'B' and a formatted string literal is prefixed with an 'f' or 'F.'

Strings can be concatenated, indexed, and sliced. In the previous example, the index for the letter 's' is b[4] because Python starts counting at 0. String indices **must be integers**. We'll look at string indices and slicing in later topics.

Strings are immutable and can not be changed. Later in this chapter, in the topic "Append to Dictionary," we look at an AttributeError caused by trying to change a string value in a dictionary. To assign a value to a string, use the same syntax and, in effect, create a new string variable with the same name. The new string has a different "identifier" and location in memory, as discussed earlier in the topic "Immutable." Strings support **concatenation**; for example, 'hello' + 'world.'

Before comparing string values, you may want to ensure both objects are of type "string," and account for uppercase and lowercase letters. The string methods **.upper()** and **.lower()** convert a string. The example below converts a variable to a string with all uppercase letters.

```
str(my_var).upper()
```

Occasionally, you may run across whitespace or a special character with an escape sequence, like the line feed '**\n**' character. The "string module" also has a function to create a list of whitespace characters. The function **repr()** displays a printable representation of a string including whitespace.

To see the methods available to a string variable, in the Console type **dir(my_str_var)**. Or, type **help(str)** for more detailed information.

String Methods

Let's take a moment to look at some of the common string methods. In a bit we'll also look at the "String Module." To see all the string methods available for your version of Python, checkout the web site docs.python.org. In the top left corner of the web site you can select your language and version, and then on the right side of the page under "Text Sequence Type -- String, click on "String Methods." After creating a string variable "mystr," in the **Console**, type "dir(mystr)" to see additional information.

Syntax	Comments
mystr.isalpha()	Returns True if all characters in the string are alphabetic (a-z) and there is at least one character.
mystr.capitalize()	Converts to Camel Case
mystr.count('39')	How often is '39' in "mystr"
mystr.find('39')	Index of first occurrence of '39'
mystr.index('9')	Returns the index for '9', or returns error if not found
mystr.isnumeric()	Returns True if all characters are number (0-9) and there is at least one character.
mystr.join(mytuple)	Creates a new string by joining an iterable (tuple, list, set, dictionary.) Elements are separated by the "mystr" value.
mystr.lower()	Change to lowercase
mystr.lstrip()	Remove whitespace on the left
mystr.rindex('9')	Same as index but counting from right
mystr.replace(old, new)	Return a copy of the string with old substring replaced by new.
mystr.rpartition(',')	Spiti or tokenize string into a tuple based on the separator ','

Syntax	Comments
mylist.rsplit(**sep='a'**)	Returns list of words in the string, using **sep** as the delimiter string. Similar to the idea of tokens in C programming.
mylist.rstrip()	Remove whitespace on the right
mylist.split(**sep='a'**)	Returns a list of words in the string, using **sep** as the delimiter string.
mystr.strip()	Return a copy of the string with the leading and trailing characters removed.
mystr.swapcase()	Return a copy of the string with uppercase characters converted to lowercase and vice versa.
mystr.upper()	Change to uppercase
mystr.zfill(**width**)	Return a copy of the string left filled with '0' digits to make the string length **width**. Think of zfill as padding numbers.

Table 6.2   String Methods

Use the **.rstrip()** method to remove characters at the end of a string.

> An example using the find() method with a string is shown in the "Find a Substring" topic that follows. The topic "Slicing" also demonstrates retrieving part of a string.

Split String

The split() function is useful for splitting strings into a "list." If no argument is given, split() assumes a space.

```
1    mystr = 'hello world'
2    mystr.split()
```

After I run the program the Console shows the value of "mystr" is a list.

```
In [2]: mystr
['hello', 'world']
```

The String Module

In addition to the built-in string methods we just looked at, there is a "string" module with several invaluable methods. The string module is useful to create strings of ASCII characters.

The next chart shows a few of the functions in the "**string**" module. In the Console, after importing the string module, you could also type "**help(string)**" to see more information.

Syntax	Comments
.ascii_letters	Both lower and uppercase letters
.ascii_lowercase	abcdefghijklmnopqrstuvwxyz
.ascii_uppercase	ABCDEFGHIJKLMNOPQRSTUVWXYZ
.digits	'012345689'
.punctuation	!"#$%&'()*+,-./:;<=>?@[\]^_`{|}~
.whitespace	` \t\n\r\x0b\x0c'
.printable	all printable characters

Table 6.3   Some String Module Methods

The **string.ascii_letters()** method is a simple way to build a list of letters. On line 1 I <u>import</u> the string module. The list() function converts the string to a list, as shown below.

```
1   import string
2
3   alphabet_string = string.ascii_letters
4   alphabet_list = list(alphabet_string)
5   print(alphabet_list)
```

Create a String of Lowercase letters

To create a string of lowercase letters use the syntax shown below. Notice in line 4 I convert the new string into a list.

```
1   import string
2   all_ltrs = string.ascii_lowercase
3   print(all_ltrs)
4   all_ltrs_list = list(all_ltrs)
5   print(all_ltrs_list)
```

After I run the program the Console shows:

In [2]:
abcdefghijklmnopqrstuvwxyz
['a', 'b', 'c', 'd', 'e', 'f', 'g', 'h', 'i', 'j', 'k', 'l', 'm', 'n', 'o', 'p', 'q', 'r', 's', 't', 'u', 'v', 'w', 'x', 'y', 'z']

Create a String of Numbers 0-9

To create a string of numbers 0-9 use the syntax shown below.

```
1   import string
2   str_Numbers = string.digits
3   print(str_Numbers)
```

After I run the program the Console shows:

In [3]:
0123456789

Whitespace Characters

To see "whitespace" characters use the **repr()** function, as shown below. On line 3, I use the repr() function to display the printable representation of the whitespace characters.

```
1   import string
2   all_ltrs = string.whitespace
3   print(repr(all_ltrs))
```

After I run the program the Console shows:

In [3]:
\t\n\r\x0b\x0c

Iterate (Loop) Through Strings

String indices must be integers. The next example of a "for" loop is perfectly legal for the loop expression, and prints the message, 'abc'

```
mystr = 'abc'
for i in mystr:
    print(mystr)
```

What happens if you want to print the string values using the index notation? The "print" statement shown below uses "i" as the index. An **error** is raised because the respective "i" values are "a", "b," and "c," and are not integers.

```
1   mystr = 'abc'
2   for i in mystr:
3       print('mystr char is:', mystr[i])
```

The **Console** displays a traceback message with a **"TypeError."** I've abbreviated the traceback message below for readability.

In [**2**]:
Traceback (most recent call last):
TypeError: string indices must be integers

A slight modification in the code would prevent the error. In the example below, I am using the "range()" function combined with the length function "len()" to get the length of the list. The range() function returns a data structure of integers. We'll look at "range" in detail later in this chapter.

```
1   mystr = 'abc'
2   for i in range(len(mystr)):
3       print('mystr char is:', mystr[i])
```

6.10 Lists

A **list** is a collection of objects. Lists are usually of the same type but can be a combination of types. A list is similar to an array in other languages and contains a sequence of elements. A unique index refers to each list item, and the index is an **integer**. When creating Lists, use square brackets **[ ]**. An index is used when updating a particular list item.

```
mylist =  ['a', 'b', 'c']
mylist[2]
```

List values are mutable which means the values **can** change. Because lists are mutable, they cannot be used as dictionary **keys**. Lists can be used as dictionary "**values**" as demonstrated later in the topic, "Append to a Dictionary." A list can grow or shrink as needed.

> Python starts counting at **0**. The first item in a list has an index of **0**, and the second item has an index of **1**.

When creating a List, use square brackets **[]**. A list will usually have homogeneous data but can mix different data types - commas separate items.

Description	Syntax	Comments
Create a List and assign values	mylist = ['a', 'b', 'c']	
Create a List and assign number values	mylist2=[1,2,3,4]	
Assign a value to the first item in the List	mylist2[0] = 8	
Access the value of the List item	mylist2[1]	Returns the value of the second item in the List
Access the value of the last List item	mylist2[-1]	Use negative index numbers when counting from the right
Return all items in a List	mylist	

Table 6.4   List Objects

Update an Element in a List

Use the index to update a particular element in a list. This example updates the second element in the list. See the topic that follows, "Index: Location of a List Element," to locate a particular index.

mylist2[1] = 8

Iterate Through Items in a List

A "for loop" is one option to iterate through items in a list, as shown below.

```
1  myList = [0, 1, 2]
2  for j in myList:
3      print('mylist item is:', myList[j])
```

Copy Lists

List copies have different behavior depending on how you make a copy of the list, as outlined in the python.org docs.

- Create a reference (same values, different identifiers)
- A shallow copy with one level

- A shallow copy with compound objects
- A deep copy

Create a Reference or Alias

The statement **mylist1** = **mylist2** creates a reference or alias. This behavior is referred to as "**indirection**." With an alias, regardless of the object name, you are actually using "mylist1." If **mylist1** has values [1, 2, 3, 4], **mylist2** references the same exact values [1, 2, 3, 4]. A change to any of the values in mylist1 is seen in mylist2, and vice versa.

Copy a Simple List

To make a copy of a list, add **[:]** at the end of the expression, as shown below. This creates a shallow copy that is one level deep. A shallow copy creates **mylist2** and inserts references to objects found in **mylist1**. You can also use the second expression to copy a list. If you leave off the **[:]** Python creates an "alias" or "reference," so that "mylist2" points to the "mylist1" object in memory.

```
mylist2 = mylist1[:]
mylist2 = list(mylist1)
```

In the case of a simple list object that is one level deep, this type of copy behaves the way you would expect. Changes at the first level are independent between the parent and copied lists, and vice versa. If you add objects to the second list, there is no change in the original list.

```
In [1]:   mylist1 = [0, 1, 2]
In [2]:   mylist2 = mylist1[:]
In [3]:   mylist2[0] = 8
In [4]: mylist1
Out[4]: [0, 1, 2]
In [5]: mylist1
Out[5]: [8, 1, 2]
```

Copy a List with Compound Objects

The same copy syntax behaves differently with compound objects. Compound objects contain other compound objects. In this next example, "mylist3" has two lists, and is two levels deep. These internal lists are shown below:

```
mylist3[0] = [1, 2, 3, 4]
mylist3[1] = ['a', 'b', 'c', 'd']
```

Here I create a shallow copy of **mylist3** called **mylist4**.

```
mylist3 = [[1, 2, 3, 4], ['a', 'b', 'c', 'd']]
mylist4 = mylist3[:]
```

The first level of mylist3 is the combined list:

[[1, 2, 3, 4], ['a', 'b', 'c', 'd']]

Changes made at the first level are independent between mylist3 and mylist4. When I replace the first level compound list mylist3[0] with a string, it has no impact on "mylist4," and vice versa.

```
In [6]:   mylist3[0] = 'hello'
In [7]:   mylist3
Out [7]: ['hello', ['a', 'b', 'c', 'd']]
In [8]:   mylist4
Out [8]: [[1, 2, 3, 4], ['a', 'b', 'c', 'd']]
```

Let's start over with mylist3 and mylist4 just after the copy that creates mylist4.

```
In [9]:   mylist3
Out [9]: [[1, 2, 3, 4], ['a', 'b', 'c', 'd']]
In [10]:   mylist4
Out [10]: [[1, 2, 3, 4], ['a', 'b', 'c', 'd']]
```

The first list object in both mylist3[0][0] and mylist4[0][0] is [1, 2, 3, 4].

The second list object in mylist3[0][1] and mylist4[0][1] is ['a', 'b', 'c', 'd'].

Now I'm going to change an object at the second level. A simple copy is only one level deep, which means changes at the second level effect both the original list **mylist3** and the copied list **mylist4**. As expected, a change to mylist4[0][2] changes mylist3[0][2], and vice versa.

```
In [11]:   mylist4[0][2] = 'z'
In [12]:   mylist4
Out [12]: [[1, 2, 'z', 4], ['a', 'b', 'c', 'd' ]]
In [13]:   mylist3
Out [13]: [[1, 2, 'z', 4], ['a', 'b', 'c', 'd' ]]
```

To avoid this shallow copy behavior with compound objects, import the "copy" library to use **copy.deepcopy()** to create a new list and insert copies of all objects in the original list. The new list is completely independent of the original list.

List Comprehension

A List comprehension is an elegant way to create a new list from a comprehension. A comprehension consists of a single expression followed by at least one for clause and zero or more for or if clauses. The only difference between a list comprehension and map() is Python returns a list instead of a map object. The comprehension is an "**expression**" followed by "**for**" loop(s) to iterate over elements. The comprehension may also include conditional "**if**" statement(s).

newList = **[expression or variable - for item in iterable- if]**

The code below has three statements that I want to combine in a "list comprehension." The list comprehension will compute sales tax for "sales_list" elements of type "float."

expression or variable	round(i * 1.065, 2)
for item in iterable	for i in sales_list
if	if type(i) == float

```
1   for i in sales_list
2       if type(i) == float:
3           round(i * 1.065, 2)
```

1. In the example below, the slash \ at the end of line 2 below means the list comprehension continues onto line 3. The Python Interpreter considers lines 2 and 3 one statement.

   On line 2, the first part of the list comprehension computes the price of items with sales tax, and rounds the result to two decimal places.

2. The second statement loops over items in the "sales_list".

3. Finally, the third statement on line 3 checks that elements are a float, skipping over strings and integers in the sales_list. The result is assigned to a new "receipt_list."

```
1   sales_list = [1, 'iPad', 399.99, 2, 'charging cable', 29.99]
2   receipt_list = [round(i * 1.065, 2) for i in sales_list \
3       if type(i) == float]
4   print(receipt_list)
```

After I run the program the Console shows the output below. Note that the first element in **sales_list** is a whole integer and not a float, so "1" is not included in the rounding calculation.

In [2]: receipt_list
Out [2]: [425.99, 31.94]

This comprehension creates a list of vowels from a string.

```
1  mystr = 'charging cable'
2  newList = [v for v in mystr if v in 'aeiou']
```

After I run the program the Console shows:

In [**2**]: newList
Out [**2**]: ['a', 'i', 'a', 'e']

Remove Characters When Converting

In the previous example, the console printed the brackets, apostrophes, and commas as part of newlist. When you convert a list to a string, the square brackets around the original list, the apostrophes, and the commas between list elements become part of the new string, as shown in the next topic, "Change a List to a String."

When converting objects, you might want to remove those extra characters. With strings, you can use the **.replace()** function to remove square brackets or commas.

The same principle applies when you convert a string object to a list. A string object begins with an apostrophe and ends with an apostrophe. The apostrophes become part of the new list element.

Delete an Item from a List

This expression uses the del() function to delete the second item in "mylist."

del(mylist[1])

In the example below, the statement "**del(mylist[4])**" deletes element 'o' from your original "mylist" object.

```
1    mylist = ['h', 'e', 'l', 'l', 'o']
2    del(mylist[4])
3    print(mylist)
```

After I run the program the **Console** shows:

```
In [2]:
['h', 'e', 'l', 'l']
```

Change a List to a String

In case you have a "list" object and need a "string" type instead, convert the list to a string using "**str(**myList**).**" In this example, I convert a list element to a string.

```
1    myList = ['hi']
2    mynewvar = str(myList)
```

After I run the program the **Console** shows:

```
In [2]: mynewvar
"['h', 'i']"
```

In the Console, type "mynewvar." The object has **double quotes** around the output, indicating the object is now a string. The **square brackets** that were around the original list object, as well as the **quotes** and **commas** that separated the original list elements are part of the value of the new string object "mynewvar."

Change a String to a List

You can convert a string to a list using "**list(**mystring**).**" You might need to convert a string to a list to change data with a "list" method, since a list is mutable and can be changed.

```
1    myList = ['hello']
2    str(mysList)
```

After I run the program the **Console** shows:

```
In [2]:  myStr
'hello'
```

6.11 Methods for Lists

In this topic, we'll look at several handy list methods. To see common sequence operations available for your version of Python, check out the **docs.python.org**. In the top left corner, you can select your language and version, and then on the left side of the page under "Sequence Types -- **list, tuple, range**, click on Mutable Sequence Types.

Syntax	Comments
mylist.append('there')	Adds an element to the end of the list
mylist.clear()	Removes all items from mylist
mylist.copy()	Creates a shallow copy of mylist (same as **newlist = mylist[:]**)
mylist.count('l')	Count occurences of 'l'
mylist.extend('you')	Add 1 element to end of list
mylist.index[1]	Returns 2nd element
mylist.insert(2, 'a')	Insert item at index location
mystring = '_'.join(mylist)	Joins list elements into a new string
mylist.pop(2)	Deletes element '2' and returns '2'
mylist.remove(2)	Removes element '2' from mylist
mylist.reverse()	Reverses the items of mylist in place
mylist.sort()	Sorts the original list & returns nothing

Table 6.5   List Methods

Append an Item to a List

The function "**append()**" adds a single element to the end of your list. Append changes your original list.

```
1    mylist = ['h', 'e', 'l', 'l', 'o']
2    mylist.append('there')
```

When I run the program the **Console** shows:

```
In [2]:
['h', 'e', 'l', 'l', 'o', 'there']
```

Extend a List, or Combine 2 Lists

The function "extend()" adds each element in the second string as a separate element to the end of the first list. In this example, when I extend the list with 'you,' it separates the letters in 'you' into three elements.

```
1    mylist = ['h', 'e', 'l', 'l', 'o']
2    mylist.extend('you')
```

When I run the program the **Console** shows:

```
In [2]:
['h', 'e', 'l', 'l', 'o', 'y', 'o', 'u']
```

Index: Location of a List Element

To find the index for the element 'e,' use the .index method. In this example, .index returns "1" which is the index for the letter 'e.' Python begins counting at "**0**," so the second element 'e' has an index of "1." Once you know the index for an element, you can change that element.

```
1    mylist = ['h', 'e', 'l', 'l', 'o']
2    mylist.index('e')
```

After I run the program the **Console** shows "1," indicating "e" is the second element in "**mylist**."

```
In [2]:
1
```

Insert an Item to a List

To add an item "a" at index position '2' in a list, use the following expression.

```
1    mylist = ['h', 'e', 'l', 'l', 'o']
2    mylist.insert(2, 'a')
```

After I run the program the Console shows:

In [2]:
['h', 'e', 'a', 'l', 'l', 'o']

Join List Elements into a String

The join() function is useful for joining elements in an iterable such as a list, tuple, dictionary, or set. In this example, I am creating a **new string** from the elements in "**mylist**." The "_" underline character is used as an argument so that the new string "**mylist2**" has "_" between each letter.

```
1    mylist = ['h', 'e', 'l', 'l', 'o']
2    mystring = '_'.join(mylist)
```

After I run the program the **Console** shows:

In [2]: mystring
h_e_l_l_o

In the next example, I join "**mylist**" elements into a string, and nothing is added between the elements.

```
1    mylist = ['h', 'e', 'l', 'l', 'o']
2    mystring = ''.join(mylist)
```

After I run the program the **Console** shows:

In [2]: mystring
'hello'

> Instead of '_', you could use '\n' to add a line feed between elements.

Add Character When Joining Strings

In the next example, I use the "map" function to change elements to a string with the str() function. Then, I join the elements together with a comma as the separator. The output to the Console when I run the program is **hi, stranger**.

```
1   mylist = ['hi', ' stranger']
2   mystr = ','.join(map(str, mylist))
3   print(myStr)
```

Pop (Remove) an Element from a List

The function **"mylist.pop()"** removes the last item in the list or the item where you provide the index. The function "pop()" also returns the item you remove.

```
1   mylist = ['h', 'e', 'l', 'l', 'o']
2   pop_item = mylist.pop(4)
3   print(pop_item)
```

After I run the program the **Console** shows:

```
In [2]:
o
```

Remove an Element from a List

The function **mylist.remove('o')** removes the argument in parentheses from a list, but does not return the object. In this example, I remove '**o**' from "**mylist**."

```
1   mylist = ['h', 'e', 'l', 'l', 'o']
2   mylist.remove('o')
3   print(mylist)
```

After I run the program the **Console** shows:

```
In [2]:
['h', 'e', 'l', 'l']
```

Remove Duplicate Elements from a List

To quickly remove duplicate elements in a list, convert the list into a **Set**.

The sort() Method

There are several ways to sort list items. The mylist.**sort**() method changes the original "mylist" into a sorted list and returns nothing.

```
1    mylist = ['h', 'e', 'l', 'l', 'o']
2    mylist.sort()
```

After I run the program the **Console** shows:

```
In [2]:
['e', 'h', 'l', 'l', 'o']
```

The sort() method also has two keyword arguments: **key** and **reverse**. The following shows two possible keyword arguments for the list.sort() method.

key=str.lower

reverse=True (reverse sort)

The sorted() Function

The "**sorted**()" function returns a new, sorted version of your list (or any iterable.) In this example, mylist2 is a new sorted list.

```
1    mylist = ['h', 'e', 'l', 'l', 'o']
2    mylist2 =sorted(mylist)
```

After I run the program the **Console** shows:

```
In [2]: mylist2
['e', 'h', 'l', 'l', 'o']
```

Sort Order and the Key Parameter

The sorted() function also has the **key** and **reverse** keyword arguments. The **reverse** keyword allows you to sort in "descending" or "ascending" order. In the next example, "reverse" is a keyword argument of the sorted() function. The **key** argument specifies a function to be called on each list element prior to making comparisons. In this example, I use the **str.lower** method to change strings to lowercase before the **sort** comparison. You could also use the **len()** function to sort words by length.

```
1    mylist = ['red', 'Red', 'blue']
2    mylist2 = sorted(mylist, key=str.lower, reverse=True)
```

Sorting by the Second Element in the List

The "operator" library includes the "itemgetter()" function which allows you to choose which element in the list you want to sort. In this example, on line 4 I am sorting by the second element and then the first element.

```
1    from operator import itemgetter
2
3    mylist = [('red', 3), ('Red', 1), ('blue', 2)]
4    mylist2 = sorted(mylist, key=itemgetter(1, 0))
```

6.12 Dictionary

A dictionary contains key:value pairs and is a non-scalar object with an internal data structure. The key:value pairs are not in any particular order, and any type of object may be used for values. Only immutable objcts can be dictionary "keys."

Dictionaries are often depicted as two columns, with the list of keys in the first column and values in the second column. Dictionaries are mutable and you can change or add key:value pairs. Values can be duplicated, but keys must be unique and hashable. You can only use immutable elements such as integers or strings as dictionary keys. While tuples can be used as dictionary keys, mutable lists can not be used as dictionary keys. I would avoid floats as keys, given the way floats are actually stored in memory.

Keys (Immutable Objects)	Values (may be any object type)
Name	John

Keys (Immutable Objects)	Values (may be any object type)
Grade	A
Course	Python Programming

Table 6.6   Sample Dictionary

A dictionary has unsorted elements that can grow and shrink as needed. When creating dictionaries, use curly braces **{}**. In the assignment statement, the key is followed by a colon **:** and a value. Each key:value pair is separated by commas.

myDict = **{**key:value, key:value, key:value**}**

The syntax for changing dictionary objects depends on the type of object in the dictionary "value." If the value is a list, you can use list methods to change data. If the value is a string, you can't change the string because strings are immutable; however, you can replace the value in the key:pair with a new object of any type.

In this section we'll explore these topics.

- Elements in a Dictionary
- Create a Dictionary
- Append to a Dictionary
- Copy a Dictionary
- How Many Elements are in a Dictionary List?
- Assign a Dictionary Value Using the Key Name
- Update a "List" Value in a Dictionary
- Find the Value of a Dictionary Item
- Find the Type of a Dictionary Element
- Add a New Key to an Existing Dictionary
- Delete a Key in an Existing Dictionary
- Iterate Through Dictionary Key-Pairs
- Iterate Through Keys in a Dictionary
- Retrieve Keys
- Search for a Key Name
- Title and Value Methods
- Combine Dictionaries

Earlier I said adding a new key:value pair to a dictionary is straightforward, but adding to an existing dictionary is not. When changing dictionary elements the important aspect is the "type" of object in the key:value pair. As you'll see in the next topic, you must know the type of the value so that you can use the corresponding methods to add or change values.

Elements in a Dictionary

This topic explores the relationship between elements in a dictionary. A dictionary is a set of key:value pairs that are not in any particular order. The keys are immutable objects like strings or integers. The values in the key:value pair can be any type of object. Often you'll see nested lists, tuples, or dictionaries in a dictionary **key:value** pair.

In the following example, we combine two lists into one "combined" list. The "combined" list will be the dictionary value. The order of elements in the two lists establishes the relationship between the two lists. The keys are student names, and the value for each student is a "combined" list that contains two lists. Recall that a dictionary is not in any kind of order, so there is no guarantee that the key "Joan" will be the first in the dictionary.

Key	Value
Joan	**[**['art', 'social studies'], ['A', 'D']**]**
Henry	**[**['math, 'english', 'science'], ['A', 'B', 'C']**]**
John	**[**['english', 'history', 'algebra'], ['B', 'B+', 'C']**]**

Table 6.7   Student Dictionary

Because dictionaries don't store data in the same order you input the data, the actual data can end up looking like the next example.

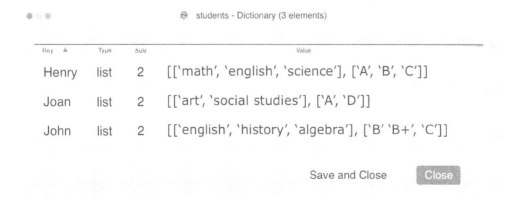

Figure 6.1   Variable Explorer Showing Dictionary

When looking at Joan's data, you can see two lists. The first course list has two elements. The second grade list also has two elements. If Joan is taking four classes, each list would have four elements.

```
['art', 'social studies']
['A', 'D']
```

The "combined" list represents the "value" for the key "Joan."

[['art', 'social studies'], ['A', 'D']**]**

When looking at this combined list, the first element in the "combined" list is a list of classes. The second element is a list of grades.

[0] -> class_list

[1] - > grade_list

We're going to create a dictionary with three students, and each student is taking several classes. Notice that we assign the list data when we create the dictionary. We don't have a separate statement to create the two lists, although we could add an additional statement for clarity.

Joan is taking art and social studies. Joan's respective grades are A and D.

```
['art', 'social studies']
['A', 'D']
```

John is taking English, history, and algebra. John's respective grades are B, B+, and C. When we create the dictionary, our class list will look like this example.

```
['english', 'history', 'algebra']
```

The grade list will look like this example.

['B', 'B+', 'C']

Henry is taking math, English, and science. Henry's respective grades are A, B, and C.

['math', 'english', 'science']
['A', 'B', 'C']

Now let's create the "students" dictionary with one student.

students = {'John': [['english', 'history', 'algebra'], ['B', 'B+', 'C']]}

At this point, let's say I want to display John's grade in his history class. I will use indexing to look at the data in this dictionary key:value pair. You can follow along with this code in your iPython Console to see the data returned. To see all of John's classes type the statement below. In this example, the first list is element [0].

students['John'][0]

To see all of John's grades type this statement. In this example, the second list is element [1].

students['John'][1]

Because dictionaries don't store data in the same order you input the data, the actual data can end up looking like the next example.

 🌑 🌑 🌑   ⋒ students - Dictionary (3 elements)

Key ▲	Type	Size	Value
Henry	list	2	[['math', 'english', 'science'], ['A', 'B', 'C']]
Joan	list	2	[['art', 'social studies'], ['A', 'D']]
John	list	2	[['english', 'history', 'algebra'], ['B' 'B+', 'C']]

Save and Close   Close

Figure 6.2   John's Grades

To see the class name 'history' type this statement. In this example, you want to see the second element [1] in the first list [0].

```
students['John'][0][1]
```

Finally, to see the class name **algebra** with John's grade, type this statement. Here we are using the third element in the first list [0][2], along with the third element in the second list [1][2].

```
print(students['John'][0][2], students['John'][1][2])
```

Recall that a dictionary assignment statement follows this syntax.

```
myDict = {key:value, key:value, key:value}
```

To create a dictionary with all students use this expression.

```
students = {'John': [['english', 'history', 'algebra'], ['B', 'B+', 'C']],
            'Henry': [['math', 'english', 'science'], ['A', 'B', 'C']],
            'Joan':[['art', 'social studies'], ['A', 'D']]}
```

To view Joan's grade in social studies, use this statement. In this example, we're looking at the second element [1] in the first list [0], and the second element[1] in the second list [1].

```
print(students['Joan'][0][1], students['Joan'][1][1])
```

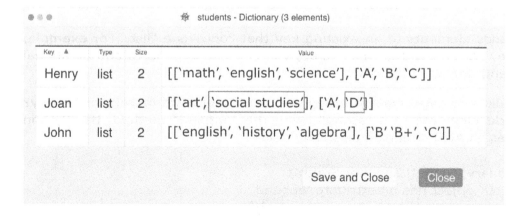

Figure 6.3   Joan's Grade in Social Studies

Create a Dictionary

To create an empty dictionary use the following expression.

mydictionary = { }

To create a dictionary with three key:pairs, use the following syntax. In the example below, the first key is 'Name,' and the value is '**Zimmerman**.' The second key is 'Grade,' and the value is '**A**.' A comma "**,**" separates the key:pairs. For readability, the key:pairs are usually written in this format. To create a dictionary with "string" values use the following syntax.

```
mydictionary = {'Name': 'Zimmerman'
            'Grade': 'A',
            'Course': 'Python Programming'}
```

In the following example, I am creating a dictionary with "list" values. Inside the "list' is a string value. Because it is a "list" there are square brackets around the string values.

```
mmydictionary2 = {'Name': ['Young']
            'Grade': ['B'],
            'Course': ['Excel Fundamentals']}
```

Because a dictionary can have any type of object, you must know the object's type in order to work with the data. Strings are contained in **quotes** (single or double), tuples use **parentheses()**, and lists use **square brackets [ ]**.

Append to a Dictionary List Value

Append adds elements to an existing key that contains a "list." For example, if you have a key "Name" with a "list" value, you can use append to add additional strings 'Smith' and 'Jones' to the "list."

Why should you care about the object type of elements in your dictionary? If you try to **add** elements to a "string" using the "append" method, the Python Interpreter raises an AttributeError, as shown below.

In [**4**]: mydictionary['Name'].append('Smith')
AttributeError: 'str' object has no attribute 'append'

The same syntax for "**mydictionary2**" is successful, because the value in the key:pair "Name" is of type "list."

In [**5**]: mydictionary2['Name'] = ['Zimmerman']
In [**6**]: mydictionary2['Name'].append('Smith')

To see the new dictionary values, in the Console, I type "mydictionary2." Notice the output shows the key "Name" now has two values. The square brackets indicate [**'Zimmerman', 'Smith'**] is a "list."

In [**6**]: mydictionary2
Out [**3**]: {'Name': ['Zimmerman', 'Smith'],
'Grade': ['A'],
'Course': ['Python Programming']}

Copy a Dictionary

Use the **.copy()** method to make a shallow copy of a dictionary.

thisdict1 = {3: 'k'}
thisdict2 = dict1.copy()

Import the "copy" library and use **copy.deepcopy()** if the dictionary contains mutable objects that can be changed.

How Many Elements are in the Dictionary List?

Continuing with the earlier example, I can count the number of values associated with the key "Name" by using the len() method to retrieve the length of the list.

In [**6**]: len(mydictionary['Name'])
Out [**3**]: 2

Assign a Dictionary Value Using the Key Name

To update a dictionary value use the following syntax.

mydictionary['Name'] = 'Smith'

Update a "List" Value in a Dictionary

There will be times when you want to "update" the value for a key in your dictionary. In this example, the key:value pair has a value that is a "list." First, I check if the key already exists in the dictionary. If the key is there, I append "myvar2" to the "list." If the key is new, I add the key and "list" value to the dictionary.

```
1  mydict = {}
2  mykey = 'phrase'
3  myvar2 = 'hello'
4  if mykey not in mydict:
5      mydict[mykey] = [myvar2]
6  else:
7      mydict[mykey].append(myvar2)
```

Next I'll use .setdefault() for the same task on line 4.

```
1  mydict = {}
2  mykey = 'phrase'
3  myvar2 = 'hello'
4  mydict.setdefault(mykey, []).append(myvar2)
```

The .get() method is another way to avoid an error if a key is not in the dictionary. The "defaultdict" object in the collections library is another way to avoid errors..

The .get() method

The collections library "defaultdict"

The .setdefault() method

Find the Value of a Dictionary Item

This example uses the **Console** to display the value of the key "Name." Compared to a list where I need to know the correct list index, with a dictionary, I simply provide the name of the "key." The Python Interpreter returns the value "Zimmerman" to the Console pane.

```
In [3]: mydictionary['Name']
'Zimmerman'
```

Keep in mind that a dictionary key:pair might contain anything. For example, the key:pair value could contain a tuple with several lists, and each list could have multiple elements. In that case, you use indexes to locate the elements that may be nested several layers into the dictionary key:pair.

To test if a particular key is in a dictionary, you could use the "in" operator. Continuing with our previous dictionary example, I might look for the keys "DoB" or "Course" with these expressions.

In [**4**]: **"DoB"** in mydictionary
Out [**4**]: False

In [**5**]: **"Course"** in mydictionary
Out [**5**]: True

Find the Type of a Dictionary Element

In case you've run across a dictionary and are wondering about the type of an object, let's look at how to find the object type. In the Editor, I've created "mydictionary2." Notice the values are in square brackets, indicating they are "lists."

```
mydictionary2 = {'Name': ['Young']
                 'Grade': ['B'],
                 'Course': ['Excel Fundamentals']}
```

After running this code in the Editor, I want to look at the type of the value in the key:pair. As shown below, in the **Console**, I use the type() function to determine the type of the value where the key is '**Name**.' The Python Interpreter returns "list."

In [**2**]: type(mydictionary2['Name'])
Out [**2**]: list

Now let's revisit the first dictionary and look at the type of the values.

```
mydictionary = {'Name': 'Zimmerman'
                'Grade': 'A',
                'Course': 'Python Programming'}
```

After running this code in the Editor, I want to look at the type of the value in the key:pair. As shown below, in the **Console**, I use the type function to determine the type of the value where the key is '**Name**.' The Python Interpreter returns "string."

In [**3**]: type(mydictionary['Name'])
Out [**3**]: str

Add a New Key:pair to an Existing Dictionary

To add a new key 'Credits' to an existing dictionary, use this syntax. Recall that you can only use <u>immutable</u> elements such as integers or strings as dictionary keys.

mydictionary['Credits'] = '3'

Delete a Key in an Existing Dictionary

To remove the key:value pair ['Credits']:'3' from the dictionary, use "del."

del**(**mydictionary['Credits']**)**

Iterate Through Dictionary Key:pair Values

This "for <u>loop</u>" returns the key:pairs in the dictionary. Line 4 in this example creates two variables, "mykey" and "myvalue," that will represent the key:value pairs. The method **items()** returns a list of the key-value pairs.

```
for mykey, myvalue in mydictionary.items():
    print("\pKey: ", mykey, "\tValue: ", myvalue )
```

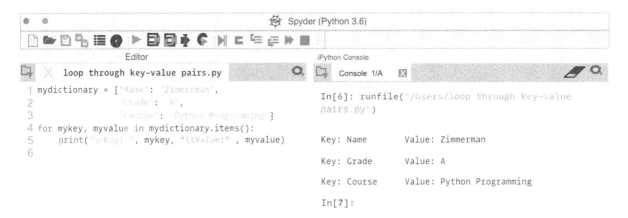

Figure 6.4   Print Key-Value Pairs

Iterate Through Keys in a Dictionary

This "for loop" returns the keys in the dictionary. To make your code easier to read, add the keys() method to the same statement.

```
for mykey in mydictionary:
    print("\pKey: ", mykey )
```

The next example is the same statement with the **.keys()** method.

```
for mykey in mydictionary.keys():
    print("\pKey: ", mykey )
```

Retrieve Keys

To retrieve the dictionary keys use the ".**keys()**" method.

In [**6**]: mydictionary**.keys()**
Out [**6**]: dict_keys(['Name','Grade', 'Course'])

Search for a Key Name

To test if a particular key is in a dictionary, you can use the "in" operator. Continuing with our previous dictionary example, I might look for the keys **"Grades"** or **"Course"** with these expressions. In this example, I am typing in the Console, and the expression returns either False or True.

In [**4**]: **"Grades"** in mydictionary
Out [**4**]: False

In [**5**]: **"Course"** in mydictionary
Out [**5**]: True

Test if Key is in the Dictionary

In another example, let's say you have a dictionary called 'mydictionary' for student IDs, where the **key** name is the student ID number. This expression that uses the "in" operator to find a student ID "12345" returns "**True**." Note I am searching for the **key** name, not the value in the key:pair.

In [**6**]: if '12345' in mydictionary:

Out [**6**]: True

Value Method

In this next example, I modified the previous code that returned the keys in the dictionary. Here I use the **value()** method to access the dictionary values. The first expression returns all values in the dictionary, while the second expression entered in the **Editor** iterates through each item.

In [**7**]: mydictionary.values()
Out [**7**]: dict_keys(['Name', 'Grade', 'Course'])

```
for myvalue in mydictionary.values():
    print(myvalue)
```

In [8]:

Combine Dictionaries

The **update()** method combines two dictionaries. If key names are the same, the key:pair is updated with the newer value. If the key:pair doesn't exist, it is added.

```
dict1, dict2 = {key1: 'data1', key2: 3}, {key3: '4'}

dict1.update(dict2)
```

Dictionary Comprehensions

Earlier, we looked at list comprehensions. Dictionaries also support comprehensions.

{expression or variable - for item in iterable- if}

```
In [16]:    myl = [1, 2, 3, 1, 3, 4, 1]
In [17]:    dd = {num: myl.count(num) for num in myl}
In [18]:    print(dd)
            {1: 3, 2: 1, 3: 2, 4: 1}
```

expression or variable   num: myl.count(num)

for item in iterable   for num in myl

Now let's look at code that reads data from an Excel file. Sample data from the Excel file is shown below.

	A	B	C
1	**Term**	**Index**	**Definition**
2	NAN	Nan	Not-a-number.
3	set	Set	A collection of objects.

This code creates a dictionary with data from columns A-C from the Excel file "words.xlsx." The "for" loop begins on line 8 and goes through line 15.

```
1   from openpyxl import load_workbook
2
3
4   wb3 = load_workbook('words.xlsx')
5   ws = wb3['words']
6   wordDict = {}
7
8   for i in range(2, ws.max_row + 1):
9       term, indx, wordDef, url = '', '', '', ''
10      term = ws.cell(i, 1).value
11      if term is not None:
12          indx = ws.cell(i, 2).value
13          wordDef = ws.cell(i, 3).value
14          if indx != '' and indx is not None:
15              wordDict[term] = [indx, wordDef]
```

The same code with lines 8-15 rewritten as a dictionary expression on lines 8-11 follows.

```
1   from openpyxl import load_workbook
2
3
4   wb3 = load_workbook('words.xlsx')
5   ws = wb3['words']
6   wordDict = {}
7
8   wordDict = {ws.cell(i, 1).value: [ws.cell(i, 2).value, ws.cell(i, 3).value]
9               for i in range(2, ws.max_row + 1):
10              if ws.cell(i, 1).value is not None and ws.cell(i, 2).value != ''
11              and ws.cell(i, 2).value is not None}
```

6.13 Range

The range function was introduced with Python 3 and is used to generate a range of **integers**. A range is immutable and can not be changed. When you run an expression with a range, the Python Interpreter creates the first integer in the range. The next integer is created when you ask for it, and so on. So you are not hampered waiting on Python to generate a large list of integers; it's more of a just-in-time approach. The format for a range is shown below.

```
for i in range(start: stop: step):
    print('Hello #', i)
```

If only one argument is provided, the argument becomes the 'stop' value. Start defaults to 0, and step defaults to 1. The range(0, 4) starts at index 0, and ends at index 3.

```
for i in range(1,4):
    print(i)
```

When I run this "for" loop from the Editor, it prints **1**, **2**, **3**, to the Console as shown below.

```
In [43]:
1
2
3
```

A range uses indexing, slicing, len(), the comparison operators "in" and "not in," and works with the "for" control loop. A range is an ideal way to iterate over a list. In the next example, the length of the list is the "stop" argument for the range() function.

```
for i in range(len(my_list)):
    print('The list item is:', my_list[i])
```

6.14 Indexes

An iterable such as a string, tuple, range, or list is a non-scalar sequence object with an internal data structure. A sequence is an iterable object that supports efficient element access using **integer** indices. These objects use indexing to locate a particular element in the sequence. The format for an index is the object name with square brackets around the index. For example, in the "bookstore" example that follows, **mystr[4]** evaluates to "s" in the string "mystr."

b	o	o	k	s	t	o	r	e
0	1	2	3	4	5	6	7	8

Table 6.8   String Index Example

In Python, the <u>sequence protocol</u> starts an index at position 0. Indexes must be integers or a TypeError occurs. In the example below, '**bookstore**' is assigned to **mystr**, and there are nine characters. The start index is [0], and the end index is [8]. If you go beyond the end of the index, it causes an "IndexError."

mystr = "**bookstore**"

0   start index

8   end index

9   length of string

To find the length of string "**mystr**" use the len() function.

In [**1**]: len(**mystr**)
Out [**1**]: 9

> len() works with many types of objects including strings, tuples, ranges, dictionaries, and lists.

Indexing is a fundamental part of Python, so we'll take a moment to look at a couple of "indexes" with data structures that have multiple levels.

Indexing Elements in Nested Lists

Earlier in the topic, "<u>Elements in a Dictionary</u>," we looked at how to index two lists inside of a dictionary. In this example, we'll look at three lists nested inside of the main list.

list1 = ['**apple**', '**tangerine**']
list2 = ['**tangy**', '**sweet**']
list3 = ['**red**', '**orange**']

mainlist = [list1, list2, list3]

The first three lists are elements [0], [1], and [2] in "mainlist." Each of the three lists has two strings, with elements [0] and [1].

To retrieve 'tangerine,' you access the second element [1] in "list1," and "list1" is the first element [0] in "mainlist."

In [1]: mainlist[0][1]
Out [1]: 'tangerine'

To view the value 'sweet,' you access the second element [1] in "list2," and "list2" is the second element [1] in "mainlist."

In [2]: mainlist[1][1]
Out [1]: 'sweet'

To view the value 'orange' you access the second element [1] in "list3," and "list3" is the third element [2] in "mainlist."

In [2]: mainlist[2][1]
Out [1]: 'orange'

Indexing Lists & Tuples in Dictionaries

These examples use strings, lists, and tuples with dictionary key:value pairs. First, I create three lists with various fruit values. The relationship between the lists is such that the first element in each list describes the "apple" - "sweet" and "red."

f1 = ['apple', 'lemon']
f2 = ['sweet', 'sour']
f3 = ['red', 'yellow']

Element	Value
f1[0]	apple
f1[1]	lemon
f2[0]	sweet
f2[1]	sour
f3[0]	red
f3[1]	yellow

Fruit Lists

In the **Console**, I can type the following to see information about the "lemon." My design is such that the data about the "lemon" is the second element [1] in lists f1, f2, and f3.

In [**1**]: f1[1]
Out [**1**]: 'lemon'

In [**2**]: f2[1]
Out [**2**]: 'sour'

In [**3**]: f3[1]
Out [**3**]: 'yellow'

Next, I create some lists for vegetable values.

v1 = ['spinach', 'carrots']
v2 = ['leafy', 'crunchy']
v3 = ['green', 'orange']

Element	Value
v1[0]	spinach
v1[1]	carrots
v2[0]	leafy
v2[1]	crunchy
v3[0]	green
v3[1]	orange

Table 6.9   Vegetable Lists

Now I create two tuples, and each tuple consists of three lists.

f = (f1, f2, f3)
v = (v1, v2, v3)

Tuple Element	Value
f[0]	f1
f[1]	f2
f[2]	f3
v[0]	v1
v[1]	v2
v[2]	v3

Table 6.10   Two Tuples

As an example, the chart below outlines the indexes for all the values in the "**f**" tuple.

Tuple (3 list elements)	List 2 string elements	Values	Tuple "f" Index
f[0]	f1[0]	apple	f[0][0]
f[0]	f1[1]	lemon	f[0][1]
f[1]	f2[0]	sweet	f[1][0]
f[1]	f2[1]	sour	f[1][1]
f[2]	f3[0]	red	f[2][0]
f[2]	f3[1]	yellow	f[2][1]

Table 6.11   Tuple Indexes

In the Console, I can type the following to see information about "lemon" in the "**f**" tuple. The layout of data is such that the data about the "lemon" is the second element [1] in each list. Because Python starts counting at zero, the second element index is [1].

```
In [1]: f[0][1]
Out [1]: 'lemon'

In [2]: f[1][1]
Out [2]: 'sour'

In [3]: f[2][1]
Out [3]: 'yellow'
```

Finally, I create a dictionary with two key:value pairs. The values are the "**f**" and "**v**" tuples. The dictionary key names are "fruit" and "vegies."

```
d = {'fruit': f, 'vegie': v}
```

Element	Value
d['fruit']	f
d['vegie']	v

Table 6.12   Dictionary

At a glance, the dictionary might look simplistic. However, when we look inside the dictionary, you see there is quite a bit of data.

Dictionary (2 tuple elements)	"f" or "v" tuples	f1,f2, f3, v1, v2, or v3 Lists	Values (strings)
d['fruit']	f[0]	f1[0]	apple
d['fruit']	f[0]	f1[0]	lemon
d['fruit']	f[1]	f2[1]	sweet

Dictionary (2 tuple elements)	"f" or "v" tuples	f1,f2, f3, v1, v2, or v3 Lists	Values (strings)
d['fruit']	f[1]	f2[1]	sour
d['fruit']	f[2]	f3[0]	red
d['fruit']	f[2]	f3[0]	yellow
d['vegie']	v[0]	v1[1]	spinach
d['vegie']	v[0]	v1[1]	carrots
d['vegie']	v[1]	v2[0]	leafy
d['vegie']	v[1]	v2[0]	crunchy
d['vegie']	v[2]	v3[1]	green
d['vegie']	v[2]	v3[1]	orange

Table 6.13   Dictionary Elements

So far, we've looked at indexing for lists and tuples. Now, I want to look at the values in the dictionary, beginning with "apple." In the **Console**, I can access the data using the dictionary key name and indexing, as shown below and in the chart that follows.

In [1]: d['fruit'][0][0]
Out [**1**]: 'apple'

In [2]: d['fruit'][1][0]
Out [**1**]: 'sweet'

In [3]: d['fruit'][2][0]
Out [**3**]: 'red'

In the previous examples, the key name is "fruit." The list '**f**' is the value in d['fruit']. List '**f**' has three lists that are index [0], [1], and [2]. I'm accessing the first element [0] in all three lists.

Dictionary Key	"f" Tuple	f1, f2, or f3" List	Values	Dictionary key name and indexes
d['fruit']	f[0]	f1[0]	apple	d['fruit'][0][0]
d['fruit']	f[0]	f1[1]	lemon	
d['fruit']	f[1]	f2[0]	sweet	d['fruit'][1][0]
d['fruit']	f[1]	f2[1]	sour	
d['fruit']	f[2]	f3[0]	red	d['fruit'][2][0]
d['fruit']	f[2]	f3[1]	yellow	

Table 6.14   Dictionary: List Indexes

6.15 Slicing

Slicing is used with strings, ranges, tuples, lists and other sequence types. "**Slicing**" breaks a sequence into a substring of elements. Notice in the example below, slicing uses square brackets **[]** and takes three arguments separated by colons. The keyword argument "start" tells the function where to start slicing the string. Start defaults to 0 and "step" defaults to 1. Both start and step are <u>optional keyword arguments</u>. If only one argument is given, it is used as the "stop" argument.

mystr[start:stop:step]

The default for the second argument "stop" is the length of the object, in this case **len(mystr)**. Using the "bookstore" string from the previous example, follow along as we look at slicing. The function **len(bookstore)** returns **9**, so the string's length is **9** characters.

b = "**bookstore**"
b[4:**9**:1]

The Console prints: **store**.

The "stop" value "**9**" evaluates to "**9** - 1." Recall that Python starts counting at 0, so this slice **b**[4:**9**:1] stops at "8" and returns characters 4-8.

The previous example equates to the following, if you were to type the <u>len()</u> function.

b[4:**len(b)**:1]

The third argument "step," tells the function which characters to return. For example, step 2 would skip every other character. "Step" can be omitted. In that case, you would type **b[4:len(b)]**. Here, the stop argument is the length of "bookstore."

The default slicing values are:

Argument	Description	Default Value
start	Start is the index to begin slicing	0
stop	The stop index where you want to stop. The default value len(b) evaluates to **stop value - 1**	len(bookstore)
step	Return every "**1**" character. (Step "**2**" skips every other character)	**1**

Table 6.15   Default Slicing Values

Slice()

The built-in <u>slice()</u> function is demonstrated in the next example. I like to use slice() to assign a name to my slices. Line 1 uses raw quotes. The "**r**" preface tells the Python Interpreter the backslash "\" isn't an escape character, but rather simply a backslash.

```
1   mystr = r"c:\data\python\Example1.py"
2   path = slice(14)
3   name = slice(15, 23)
4   extension = slice(24, 26)
5   print(mystr[path])
6   print(mystr[name)
7   print(mystr[extension])
```

On line 2, there is one **slice()** argument, which is the "stop" value. On line 3 and 4, I use both the start and stop arguments. The output from lines 5-7 is shown below.

```
c:\data\python
Example1
py
```

Slicing Examples

This example b**[0:4]** evaluates to **book**. The Python Interpreter starts at "0" and ends at "3."

b[0:4]								
b	o	o	k	s	t	o	r	e
0	1	2	3	4	5	6	7	8

The next example b**[4:]** evaluates to **store** because only the '4' start argument is provided. If you don't provide a "stop" argument, the default of **len(bookstore)** is used.

b[4:]								
b	o	o	k	**s**	**t**	**o**	**r**	**e**
0	1	2	3	4	5	6	7	8

Don't forget the colon at the end of the start argument!

Notice the example below b[4] looks similar to the previous example but omits the colon. Now Python returns only the character "**s**" at index **4**.

b[4]								
b	o	o	k	**s**	t	o	r	e
0	1	2	3	**4**	5	6	7	8

Negative values tell Python to start counting from the right. The example below **b[::-1]** evaluates to:

erotskoob

b[:: -1]								
b	**o**	**o**	**k**	**s**	**t**	**o**	**r**	**e**
0	1	2	3	4	5	6	7	8

In this example **b[5:2:-1]**, the "-1" step argument tells the Python Interpreter to move right to left. This example starts at "5," steps right to left because of "-1", and stops before index "2" at "k":

tsk

b[5:2: -1]								
b	o	o	**k**	**s**	**t**	o	r	e
0	1	2	3	4	5	6	7	8

In this example b[**-8**:**-3**:] a negative start argument "**-8**" counts from right to left, beginning with "**o**." There is no step argument, so the default of "**1**" is used, meaning you move left to right, from **-8** to **-7** to **-6**, and so on. The stop argument is "**-3**," telling Python to stop before it reaches **-3**. This slice evaluates to:

ookst

b[-8:-3:]								
b	**o**	**o**	**k**	**s**	**t**	o	r	e
-9	**-8**	**-7**	**-6**	**-5**	**-4**	-3	-2	-1

The last example, **b[-7:2:-1]** below, evaluates to an empty string because it goes beyond the end of the string. It starts at -7, moves to -8, and then -9. At that point, it has moved three indices from right to left and can't move anymore.

b[-7:2: -1]								
b	o	o	k	s	t	o	r	e
-9	-8	-7	-6	-5	-4	-3	-2	-1

> In the topic "Find a Substring" that follows, we'll use slicing to find the word "from" in a string.

6.16 Operators

Now let's take a look at using operators for numerical operations, concatenation, and comparisons. The **docs.python.org** has a complete list of operators in the topic "Mapping Operators to Functions."

Numerical Operators

Arithmetic operators work pretty much the way you would expect in Python.

Operator	Example	Description
+	x + y	the sum
-	x - y	the difference
+=	x += 1	add 1
-=	x -= 1	minus 1
*	x * y	the product

Operator	Example	Description
/	x / y	division
//	x // y	floor division: **5 // 2** returns 2
%	x%y	modulo: the remainder when x is divided by y
**	i**j	i to the power of j or exponentiation

Table 6.16   Numerical Operators

These two statements both add 1 to the **mynumber** variable.

```
mynumber = mynumber + 1
mynumber += 1
```

Select Odd or Even Numbers

One way to select odd or even index numbers is to use "**+=**". Given that the first element in a tuple is mytuple1[0], I can increment a counter += 2 to iterate through all the even index elements in the tuple. The following example creates a new tuple with the first element, third element, and fifth elements from "**mytuple1**."

```
1   myTuple1 = (1, 2, 3, 4, 5)
2   myTuple2 = ()
3   i = 1
4   while i < len(myTuple1):
5           myTuple2 += (myTuple1[i],)
6       i += 2
7   print(myTuple2)
```

Modulo Operator

The "**modulo**" operator "**%**" returns the remainder when dividing two numbers. If you divide any number by 10, the modulo is the last digit in a number. This example returns '7' in the Console.

```
In [1]: n = 107
In [2]: last_digit = n % 100
In [3]: print(last_digit)
7
```

Select Odd or Even Numbers

You'll often see the remainder "%" operator used to identify odd or even numbers, as shown below.

```
for i in range(0, 20):
if i % 2 != 0:
    print("i is an odd number", i)
```

Integer Division

The '$//$' operator does integer division also known as floor division. Integer division returns the quotient and ignores the remainder. This example returns '12' in the Console, in effect reducing the original number by one digit.

```
In [1]: n = 123
In [2]: myvar = n // 10
In [3]: print(myvar)
12
```

Concatenation, Repetition and Sequence Operations

The **+** operator is used to concatenate string objects. You can also use the + operator to concatenate two lists and other object types.

The * repetition operator is supported by most sequence types. An example of repetition is **3 * 'ho'**, which evaluates to "ho ho ho."

To see common sequence operations available for your version of Python, check out the **docs.python.org**. In the top left corner, you can select your language and version, and then on the left side of the page under, "Sequence Types, click on "Common Sequence Operations."

Operator	Description
len(s)	length of s
min(s)	smallest item of s
max(s)	largest item of s
s.count(x)	total number of occurances of x in s

Comparison Operators

Use Comparison Operators to compare two values. The "in" and "not in" operators are handy for searching or finding elements in a data structure.

Operator	Description
in	Test for <u>membership</u> in a sequence
not in	Returns True if not a member of a sequence

To test whether a **character** or **substring** is in a string, use the "in" comparison operator, as shown below.

```
mystr = 'apple'
if 'a' in mystr:
    print('a is in', mystr)
```

In the previous example, I searched for the string "a" in "mystr." The left operand and the right operand are both strings. A TypeError is raised if you use a "list" as the left operand and a string as the right operand.

The "in" comparison operator is used with strings, tuples, ranges, and lists.

Boolean Operations

The <u>boolean operators</u> are "and," "or," and "not" and are sometimes referred to as <u>short-circuit operators</u>. The evaluation of a compound <u>boolean</u> expression stops when an outcome is reached. In this example, the Python Interpreter stops evaluating the expression after the argument "5 == 4" evaluates to "False."

if 5 == 4 and 2 != 6:

Identity Comparison

The "**is**" and "**is not**" operators test an object's identity. If "x" and "y" variables point to the same object <u>identifier</u> "x **is** y" returns True. This next statement returns "True."

5 **is not** 4

Let's say you create a variable "myvar1" and assign the value "hello." You then create a new variable, "myvar2," and assign it to "myvar1" with the statement myvar2 = myvar1. In effect, you create an "alias" from "myvar2" to "myvar1". The two statements below return "True" because the objects are the same.

myvar1 == myvar2

myvar1 is myvar2

You could also use the id() function to verify these two variables point to the same object. In this example, notice the identifier is the same.

```
In [14]: id(myvar1)
Out [14]: 140498313577904
In [15]: id(myvar2)
Out [15]: 140498313577904
```

Comparison Operators

Operator	Description
>	Greater than
<	Less than
>=	Greater than or equal to
<=	Less than or equal to
==	Equal (values)
!=	Not equal

Table 6.17   Comparison Operators

Difference Operator

Earlier, in the Sets topic, we looked at the difference operator - dash. This creates a new set with the elements in "myset1" that are **not** in "myset2."

```
In [21]:    myset1 = {1, 2, 3}
In [22]:    myset2 = {3, 4, 5}
In [23]:    myset1 - myset2
Out[23]:    {1, 2}
```

The Union Operator for Sets

Earlier in the "Sets" topic we looked at the "union" | operator to combine two sets.

Comparing Floats

Non-integer numbers, or floats, are stored in computer memory as a binary representation of 0's and 1's. Calculations can introduce subtle differences where you may think both float values are 1.08, but the actual binary representation is slightly different. Comparing two floats, as shown below, could potentially return **False**.

```
x == y
```

Instead of the == equals comparison for floats, use an arbitrarily small positive number (an epsilon) to compare two floats. In the next statement, the epsilon is .000001, and the statement returns 'True' if the float values are within .000001 of each other, which is good enough for this example. The **abs()** function converts floats to positive numbers for the comparison.

```
if abs(x-y) < .000001:
```

See the cmath library function **isclose()** for comparing floats.

Comparisons that Return True or False

When you compare two objects, the Python Interpreter returns "True" if the comparison is "True" or "False" if the comparison is not True. In the Console type the following statement. Python returns "True."

```
In [1]: 'apple' == 'apple'
Out [1]: True
```

The next two functions both return "True". Because the second function "**myfunction2**" is simpler, it is considered more "Pythonic."

```
def myfunction():
    if 2 == 2:
        return True
```

```
def myfunction2():
    return 2 == 2

print(myfunction())
print(myfunction2())
```

Bitwise Operators

The ampersand **&** bitwise <u>operator</u> copies a bit if it exists in both operands. In this example, the bitwise operator **&** returns a new set with the elements in common between the two sets. The symmetric_difference() function also returns common objects.

```
In [18]:     myset1 = {1, 2, 3}
In [19]:     myset2 = {3, 4, 5}
In [20]:     myset1 & myset2
Out[20]:    {3}
```

The next example uses the bitwise **exclusive** or ^ carat operator to create a new set with the elements **not** in common between the two sets.

```
In [21]:     myset1 = {1, 2, 3}
In [22]:     myset2 = {3, 4, 5}
In [23]:     myset1 ^ myset2
Out[23]:    {1, 2, 4, 5}
```

The bitwise **|** pipe operator returns a set of **all** objects.

```
In [21]:     myset1 = {1, 2, 3}
In [22]:     myset2 = {3, 4, 5}
In [23]:     myset1 | myset2
Out[23]:    {1, 2, 3, 4, 5}
```

Find a Substring

Earlier we looked at <u>slicing</u> which is a simple way to parse a string into substrings. In the next example, I use the find() method to locate all instances of the substring "**from**." I'm using a "**start**" variable for the beginning of the string and a "**stop**" variable for the end of the string.

1. As I loop through the code, each time I find a match on line 7, I print the value on line 10.

2. On line 8, I update the stop value. I am searching for "from" which has 4 characters.

3. To continue searching the remaining string, I reset the **start** value on line 12.

4. On line 11, I update "search_str" to reflect the "remaining" string.

```
1    original_str = "the apple fell far from the tree"
2    found_str = ''
3    search_str = original_str
4    start = 0
5    while start < len(original_str):
6        start = search_str.find('from')
7        if start != -1:
8            stop = start + 4
9            found_str = search_str[start:stop]
10           print(found_str)
11           search_str = search_str[stop:]
12           start = 0
13       else:
14           break
```

Find Last Element in a String

This next example uses the split() method to search a string for a ` ` space, and then uses slicing to return the last word in the string.

```
In [16]: my_str = "the apple fell far from the tree"
In [17]: print(my_str.split('')[-1])
Out[16]: tree
```

The next example uses the **.rindex()** method to return the start index of the last list element. In this example, the **stop index** in the square brackets **[ ]** is set by **[my_str.rindex(` ')]**.

```
In [18]: print(my_str[my_str.rindex(` ')])
Out [18]: tree
```

6.17 Identifiers

Classes identified by patterns of leading and trailing underscore characters have special meanings.

Interactive Interpreter

The special identifier "_" underscore is used in the interactive interpreter (or Console) to store the result of the last evaluation.

Class-Private Names

Within the context of a class definition, class-private names are often renamed to avoid clashes between "private" attributes of base and derived classes. For example, a private class variable/method/class may begin with an underscore.

System-Defined Names

Special method names refer to system-defined or "dunder" names. These **"special method names"** begin and end with two underline characters. These methods are invoked by special syntax, such as arithmetic operators or subscripting and slicing. This is Python's approach to *operator overloading*.

__add__

__enter__

__eq__

__exit__

__hash__

__init__

__len__

__lt__

__main__

__name__

__new__

__str__

__sub__

__version__

A module's **__name__** is set equal to '**__main__**' when read from standard input, a script, or from an interactive prompt. Top-level code executes at the '**__main__**' scope, as outlined at docs.python.org. A module can discover whether or not it is running in the main scope by checking its own __name__.

In the **Console**, type the module name plus **.__version__** to view the version of the module, as shown below.

openpyxl.__version__

The name of the class is found in the **.__name__** method.

openpyxl.__name__

A "**with statement**" uses the context management protocol that requires the **__enter__** and **__exit__** methods. PEP343 defines a "with statement" that wraps the execution of a block of code with methods defined by the context manager. The most common uses of a "with statement" are for file handling or network ports.

6.18 Compound & Conditional Statements

Python compound statements control the flow of the program. Compound statements begin with for, while, if, else, try, or with. When the control statement is **True**, the indented lines that follow run.

- for
- while
- if
- else

The control statement always ends with a colon : and you indent the next line of code to the right. If you want to run several lines of code as part of the control statement, the lines are all indented.

The first line of the control statement, and all the indented lines that follow, are called a "Suite" in Python. Other programming languages often refer to this structure as a block of code. A statement is part of a suite (a "block" of code). A statement is either an expression or one of several constructs with a keyword, such as if, while or for. The next topic looks at suites.

> The "for" control statement is used with objects like strings, tuples, ranges, and lists.

Conditional Expression

The simple conditional expression below returns "x" if **C** is true, otherwise it returns "y".

```
x if C else y
```

To demonstrate an if-else expression searching for letters, this example returns 'Found' because "h" is in "hi".

```
'Found' if "h" in "hi" else 'not found'
```

The next example of an "if" statement returns True.

```
myvar = 'world'
if myvar:
    print('myvar has a value')
```

For Loop

A "for" or "while" loop repeats itself until a condition is met. The condition might be the end of an iterable list, or when a conditional statement is False. The

Python Interpreter evaluates the statement and continues executing that block of code if the statement is True. If the statement is False, the loop ends.

```
for i in range(0, 20):
if i % 2 != 0:
        print("i is an odd number", i)
```

The next "for loop" iterates or moves through items in a data structure. When this program runs, each time the program loops through the code, the next item in the list is displayed.

To see a **for** loop in action, type this code in your **Editor** window, then click run.

```
fruits = ['Apple','Orange', 'Watermelon']
for fruit in fruits:
        print('my fruit is:', fruit)
```

The output of this code is shown below.

```
my fruit is:  Apple
            my fruit is:  Orange
            my fruit is:  Watermelon
```

Continue Until Break

In another example, the statement below is always **True**, so the program runs until you break out of the loop.

while **True**:

In the next example, the "while" code block runs as long as "myvar" has a value. When "myvar" has no value, the code on lines 4-5 runs. Line 5 breaks out of the loop.

```
1    myvar = 'some value'
2    while True:
3        if not myvar:
4            print('myvar is blank so break')
5            break
6        for i in range(3):
7            print('i is ', i, ' and myvar is ', myvar)
8            if i == 2:
9                myvar = ''
```

Iterables

An iteration variable can also be used to iterate through elements in a container. A container could be a list, tuple, or dictionary, As an example of an iterator, in the code that follows the variable "i" is a number with the default starting value of "0." The first time the loop runs, list[i] refers to list[0]. As the program loops, the next time the list runs, list[i] refers to list[1].

```
fruits = ['Apple', 'Orange', 'Watermelon']
for i in range(3):
    print('my fruit is:', fruits[i])
```

The output of this code is shown below.

my fruit is: Apple

my fruit is: Orange

my fruit is: Watermelon

A **StopIteration** error is raised to indicate the end of an iterator.

---

iter()

The iter() function from the itertools library has two very different behaviors. If the function call **iter(mylist)** includes one argument, like a list, the function iterates over the list. When you pass only one argument, **iter()** expects a collection object that supports the iterator protocol or sequence protocol. If a second argument, *sentinel*, is given, the object must be a callable object, like a function. Later in this chapter, in the "Function" topic, we'll look at

iter(myfunction, *sentinel***).**

The itertools library has some other interesting functions, like chain() that iterates over two containers in one function call.

6.19 Indented Code (a Suite)

In Python, the first line of a control statement, and all the <u>indented</u> lines that follow, are called a "Suite" of code. In the next figure, there is a red box around the code from line 28 to 48. I added a red vertical dotted line to highlight where the code is indented.

Let's look at the code on lines 29, 30, 31, 32, and 48. These lines are all indented to the same vertical level. This code Suite, or block of code, begins on line 28. The last line in this code Suite is line 48.

Indentation in Python scripts defines a "Suite" or code block.

In this example, the shaded Suite (block of code) is a second "while loop" (lines 32 to 46.) This second Suite is "nested" because it is inside the first Suite. Within the nested Suite, line 38 only runs when the **if statement** on line 37 evaluates to "**True**." A nested "if statement" means there is a second "if statement" within the first "if statement."

In this example, the "**bfr**" counter on line 48 is the last line in this Suite and, in effect, moves forward in the loop to the next item.

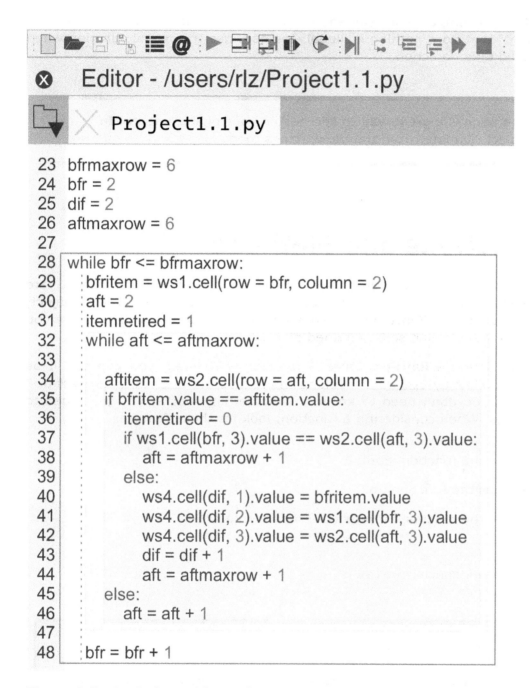

```
23  bfrmaxrow = 6
24  bfr = 2
25  dif = 2
26  aftmaxrow = 6
27
28  while bfr <= bfrmaxrow:
29      bfritem = ws1.cell(row = bfr, column = 2)
30      aft = 2
31      itemretired = 1
32      while aft <= aftmaxrow:
33
34          aftitem = ws2.cell(row = aft, column = 2)
35          if bfritem.value == aftitem.value:
36              itemretired = 0
37              if ws1.cell(bfr, 3).value == ws2.cell(aft, 3).value:
38                  aft = aftmaxrow + 1
39              else:
40                  ws4.cell(dif, 1).value = bfritem.value
41                  ws4.cell(dif, 2).value = ws1.cell(bfr, 3).value
42                  ws4.cell(dif, 3).value = ws2.cell(aft, 3).value
43                  dif = dif + 1
44                  aft = aftmaxrow + 1
45          else:
46              aft = aft + 1
47
48      bfr = bfr + 1
```

Figure 6.5   An Indented "Suite" or Block of Code

In Python, an empty Suite (indented block of code) is illegal. For example, an "if statement" that does nothing is illegal. Instead, use the "pass" function when your code should take no action.

The Outline pane is a great way to see nested control statements. In Spyder, select "Outline" from the View, Panes menu.

6.20 Functions and Methods

Functions are a sequence of statements. Python functions are first-class objects, which means functions are treated like any other type of object, such as integers or tuples. Functions are an example of **decomposition**, where you break a program into smaller, self-contained pieces.

First, you define a function. Once a function is defined, you can use it as many times as you like by calling or invoking the function. The term "**Abstraction**" refers to the fact you don't need to know how something works, you just need to know what it does. When considering a function, look for these features.

1.   What are the function inputs?

2.   What does the function do?

3.   What are the function outputs (the return object?)

```
1    def menu(meal, special=False):
2        <some code>
```

When you define a function within a class, it is called a **method**.

Depending on whether you are defining or calling a function, you call the items in parentheses either "parameters" or "arguments." When defining a function, the items in parenthesis are **parameters**. When calling a function, the items are **arguments**.

Defining a Function

When defining a function in the **Editor,** the parameters in parentheses specify what types of arguments (objects) the function can accept. In this example, the parameter "special" assigned a default boolean value of "False."

```
1   def menu(meal, special=False):
2       msg = ""
3       if special is True:
4           msg = 'The specials today are Mimosas. '
5       if meal == 'breakfast':
6           msg = 'Breakfast is eggs and toast. '
8       else:
9           msg = 'Sorry, we ran out of food. '
10      return msg
```

The parameter "meal" has no default value. Because of Python's dynamic typing, when calling the function, I can pass any type of data for "meal."

The Python style guide recommends function names begin with a lowercase letter. Class names should begin with an uppercase letter.

The **signature()** function tells you what parameters another function expects, what that function does, and the function's return object.

Calling or Invoking a Function or Method

When calling or invoking a function, you pass arguments with values to the function inside the parenthesis. If there are no arguments, the parenthesis are empty but are still required to indicate the function call. In the example below, the last line calls the function "**menu.**"

```
1   def menu(meal, special=False):
2       msg = ""
3       if special is True:
4           msg = 'The specials today are Mimosas. '
5       if meal == 'breakfast':
```

```
 6              msg = 'Breakfast is eggs and toast. '
 8         else:
 9              msg = 'Sorry, we ran out of food. '
10         return msg
11 print(menu('breakfast'))
```

The two statements below call the "menu" function and produce the same result. In the second example, I omit the optional keyword argument. When calling the function, the parameter "meal" is referred to as a positional argument that has a value of "**breakfast**."

```
menu('breakfast', special = False)
menu('breakfast')
```

Parameters

In the previous example, there are two parameters in the function definition, "meal" and "special."

	Parameter Name	Default Value	Required/Optional
Positional	meal		Required
Keyword	special	False	Optional

Table 6.18   Parameters

Arguments

Arguments are the values you pass to a function when calling the function. Not all functions have arguments. In this example, the function call has two arguments.

menu('breakfast', special=True)

Order	Parameter Name	Argument Value
1	meal	breakfast
2	special	True

Table 6.19   Arguments

When I call this function, the parameters are now referred to as "arguments" because I am calling the function.

Keyword (Optional) Arguments

PEP 3102 defines keyword arguments which are optional because there is a default value in the function definition. When calling a function, a name or "keyword" precedes the keyword argument. The second parameter in my earlier function definition includes the **keyword** "special" with a default value of "False."

Positional Arguments

The "meal" argument is a positional argument because it does not have a keyword and default value. Positional arguments are mandatory or required since there is no default value. You must list **positional arguments** before any **keyword arguments**. The example below is **invalid** because a positional argument is after a keyword argument.

def **menu**(special=False, meal):

In the previous example of the menu() function, the "special" argument has a default value. When calling the menu() function, "special" is an **optional** argument. If you don't provide the argument when calling this function, Python uses the default value "False" specified in this function's definition.

If a function has optional keyword arguments with default values, the values are assigned using the "scope" that exists at the time of the function definition. The global scope is used in the previous example where the menu() function definition is on line 1. In the case of nested functions, the function definition might be in the enclosing scope, as shown at the end of this Chapter in the namespace topic.

> An optional argument with a default value is another way to implement the concept of a "global variable." Let's say you want a running "total" value. The first time you call the function, you set the optional argument "total=0". Within the function, you update the total value. As you make recursive function calls, you pass the latest "total" value as an argument to the recursive function call statement.

Unpacking Operator Arguments

Occasionally, you may need to set an arbitrary number of arguments for a function. In the function definition, an asterisk * prefaces arguments to indicate the function can use an arbitrary number of objects. A variable number of positional arguments is often shown as myfunction(*args) and a variable number of keyword arguments is shown as myfunction(*kwargs).

Let's say you have a function that prints personalized movie tickets for each patron. The patron names vary from day-to-day. In the next code example, on line 1, there are two **parameters** enclosed in parenthesis:

```
1  def print_tickets(number_of_tickets, *name):
2      i = 0
3      while i < number_of_tickets:
4          print(name[i])
5          i += 1
6
7  print_tickets(2, 'John', 'Alice')
```

The function definition on line 1 includes an asterisk * or "unpacking operator" to indicate there is an arbitrary number of **name** arguments passed to the function. For more information on unpacking operators, see the next sections. There are two paramters in the function definition.

> number_of_tickets
>
> *****name**

When I call the function on line 7, I pass it three arguments. Two of the arguments are names.

print_tickets(2, 'John', 'Alice')

Unpacking Operators

PEP 448 defines "Additional Unpacking Generalizations." You can define functions to take *x and **y arguments. Unpacking operators allow a function to accept any number of arguments that aren't specifically named in the declaration.

The asterisk * or 'iterable unpacking operator' unpacks the iterable into positional arguments.

The double asterisk ** or 'dictionary unpacking operator' provides the same behavior for dictionaries. You can pass arguments stored in a dictionary to a function using **, as shown below. This example is an arbitrary keyword argument dictionary.

```
In [1]: kwargs = {color: 'blue', height: 4}
In [2]: myfunction(**kwargs)
```

To pass arguments stored in an iterable to a function, use the * unpacking operator. An iterable might be a list or tuple. This example uses the "names" list to provide the arbitrary positional arguments.

```
In [1]: names = ['John', 'Alice']
In [2]: print_tickets(2, *names)
```

If you leave off the * unpacking operator in the function call on line 2, an error is raised.

The PEP 3132 "Extended Iterable Unpacking" specifies a "catch-all" name which is assigned to a list of all items not assigned to a "regular" name. In the next example, an asterisk * indicates "b" is assigned all remaining values.

```
1    a, *b = (1, 2, 3, 4)
```

The result is "a" = 1 and "b" is a tuple: (2, 3, 4).

How to View the Function Argument Definition

To view arguments accepted by a function or method, you can use the help() function or inspect the function's **call signature**. For example, to see the arguments of the meal() function, run the program to create the function. In the **Console**, import the inspect library, and type the print statement shown below. The Python Interpreter returns the parameters for the menu function.

```
In [4]: from inspect import signature
In [5]: print(str(signature(menu)))
(meal, special=False)
```

An **AttributeError** is raised if there is a missing keyword name when calling a method.

The devguide.python.org has details of the style guide for Python's documentation, and PEP 257 is specific to docstrings.

Function Return or Yield Objects

A function "returns" or "yields" one object; however, that object might be a container like a tuple with several items. When a function doesn't specify a return value, it returns the special value "NoneType" discussed earlier. As the Python Interpreter moves through the code in a function, when it encounters the keyword "return," it stops execution and returns the value in the return expression. Nothing after the return statement is executed.

> When a function uses the 'yield' statement instead of the 'return' statement, the function is a **generator**, as discussed previously.

For debugging purposes, let's look at the function return object in terms of:

- What **type** of return object does the function return?
- Does the function return a value of "**None**?"
- Does the function return a tuple with several items?

This function returns a tuple with three strings and an int. When I call the function on line 6, I pass the return tuple elements to my variables "mystr1", "mystr2", "myint", and "mystr3".

```
1  def myfunction():
2      print('hi')
3      return 'str1', 'str2', 5, 'str3'
4
5
6  mystr1, mystr2, myint, mystr3 = myfunction()
```

Once I run the code, and the function definition is created, I can use the "type()" function in the Console to find what type of object the function returns.

In [3]: type(myfunction())

Out [3]: tuple

> The absence of a function return object may cause an error, if the original **function call** expects a function return object. When debugging you might comment all code in a function, and an error still occurs because of a discrepancy in the return object.

Boolean Return Object

The next two functions both return "True." Because the second function, "**myfunction2**" is simpler, it is considered more "Pythonic."

```
def myfunction():
    if 2 == 2:
        return True

def myfunction2():
    return 2 == 2
```

Return the Statement that is True

The next example of a return statement would return the value of "y" or 'hello' because Python returns the True statement. It is "True" that **y** is a string; and "False" that **x** is an integer. In this case, whichever expression is "True" would be returned.

```
x = 'john'

y = 'hello'

return isinstance(x, int) or isinstance (y, str)
```

All Paths Do Not Have a Return Value

Previously, the "menu" function returned a value on line 10. A return value **must exist for all paths** through the function. In the next example, I modified the program to have different return values for several paths. The "if" suites of code on lines 3-5 and 6-10 both have return values.

```
1   def menu(meal, special=False):
2       msg = ""
3       if special is True:
4           msg = 'The specials today are Mimosas. '
5           return msg
6       if meal == 'breakfast':
7           msg = 'Breakfast is eggs and toast. '
8           return msg
9       else:
10          msg = 'Sorry, we ran out of food. '
```

```
11  print(menu('lunch'))
```

Do you see the problem with this code? The "else" suite of code beginning on line 9 does not have a return value. When there is no return value, the Python Interpreter returns the value "**None**," which may not be what you wanted.

Index Example for a Tuple Return Object

In the next example, on line 12 I pass the function's return values to **mytxt**. Because the function returns two values on line 9, "**mytxt**" is now a tuple. When I try to print **mytxt** on line 16, the Console displays an **error**.

```
1   def menu(meal, special=False):
2       msg, msg2 = "", "Thank you."
3       if special is True:
4           msg = 'The specials today are Mimosas. `
5       if meal == 'breakfast':
6           msg = 'Breakfast is eggs and toast. '
7       else:
8           msg = 'Sorry, we ran out of food.'
9           return msg, msg2
10
11
12  mytxt = menu('lunch')
13  if mytxt is None:
14      pass
15  else:
16      print(mytxt)
```

To fix my program, I need to change line 18 to print each element in the "**mytxt**" tuple, as shown below. The variable "mytxt" is now a tuple, so I may want to rename the variable.

```
print(mytxt[0], mytxt[1])
```

The Type of Return Value

The type of return value is important if you're using it as the argument for another function. In the earlier example, the "print" function expects a string, and my "**menu**" function returns a tuple. In this new example, the Python Interpreter raises an error. Using the previous function as an example, in the **Console**, I could use the function "type" to identify the type of object the "**menu**" function returns.

```
In [1]: myTuple = (msg, msg2)
In [2]: type(myTuple)
Out [2]: tuple
```

Recursive Functions

A recursive function calls itself until a statement, or base case, terminates the function. Typically a recursive call solves problems at a high level, reducing the problem's size at each recursive call, until finally, you reach your base case, which is the simplest form of the problem. The recursive call terminates at your base case. The solution to the "Towers of Hanoi" is a famous example of a recursive problem.

In the next example, the function calls itself recursively on line 5 until **bookcnt** is more than the length of "books" on line 2. If you omit the termination expression on line 2, the program runs continuously until a **RecursiveError** is eventually raised.

```
1   def printbooks(books, bookcnt=0):
2       while bookcnt < len(books):
3           print(books[bookcnt])
4           bookcnt += 1
5           bookcnt = printbooks(books, bookcnt)
6       return bookcnt
7
8
9   books = ['bk1', 'bk2', 'bk3']
10  cnt = int(printbooks(books))
11  print('There are %d books in %s' % (cnt, books))
```

Recursive Memory Stacks

This topic looks at what happens with memory stacks as you make recursive calls. The code below includes a function "c" and a recursive call within the function on line 10.

```
1   def c(b, bc=0):
2        i = '\nStack'
3        j = ' - bc value is'
4        k = "'bc' identifier is "
5        while bc < len(b):
6            bc += 1
7            i = i + str(bc + 1) + j + str(bc)
8            print(i)
9            print(k, id(bc))
10           bc = c(b, bc)
11       return bc
12
13
14  books = ['bk1', 'bk2', 'bk3']
15  print('\nStack 1 (global namespace)')
16  cnt = c(books)
17  print('\nThere are %d books in %s' % (cnt, books))
```

When I run the program, the **Console** outputs the following.

Stack 1 (global namespace)

Stack2 - bc value is 1
'bc' identifier is 4485190800

Stack3 - bc value is 2
'bc' identifier is 4485190832

Stack4 - bc value is 3
'bc' identifier is 4485190864

There are 3 books in ['bk1', 'bk2', 'bk3']

Let's look at a visual picture of how the Python Interpreter moves up and down the stacks.

When the program initially runs, it creates the global namespace or **Stack 1**. Line 16 calls the function **c()** and creates memory **Stack 2**. In memory **Stack 2**, after the program runs line 6, my counter "bc" has a value of 1, and the identifier for "bc" is 4485190800. On line 10, the program makes a recursive call to function **c()** and creates memory **Stack 3**.

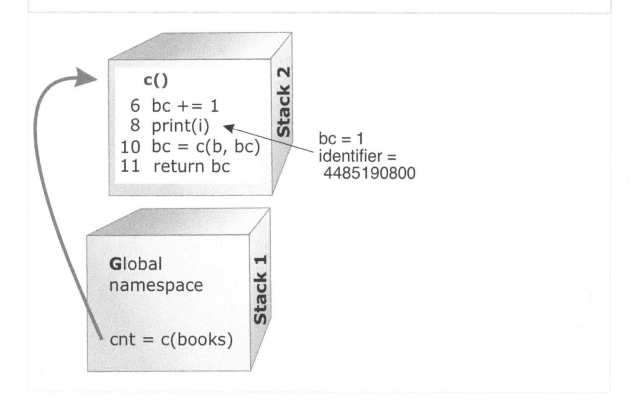

In memory **Stack 3**, after the program runs line 6 again, "bc" has a value of 2, and the identifier for "bc" is 4485190832. While "bc" has the same name, the identifiers are different, indicating these are two different variables. On line 10, the program makes a recursive call to function **c()** and creates memory **Stack 4**.

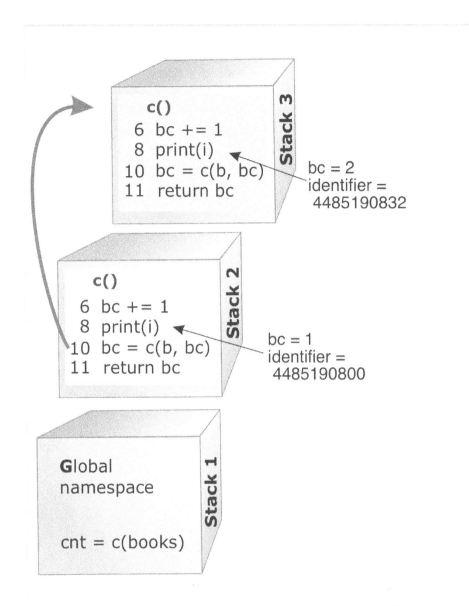

c()
6 bc += 1
8 print(i)
10 bc = c(b, bc)
11 return bc

bc = 2
identifier =
    4485190832

c()
6 bc += 1
8 print(i)
10 bc = c(b, bc)
11 return bc

bc = 1
identifier =
    4485190800

Global
namespace

cnt = c(books)

Stack 3

Stack 2

Stack 1

In memory **Stack 4**, the program again runs line 6. Now "bc" has a value of 3, and the identifier is 4485190864. On line 10, the program makes a recursive call to function **c()** and creates memory **Stack 5**.

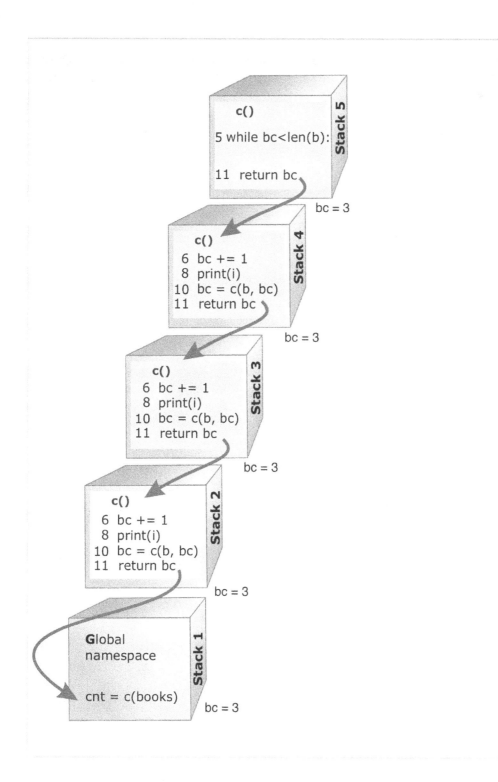

In memory **Stack 5**, when line 5 compares the value of bc to the length of "b," the Python Interpreter returns False. At this point, "bc" has a value of 3, and the length of "b" is 3.

line 5: 3 < 3 is False

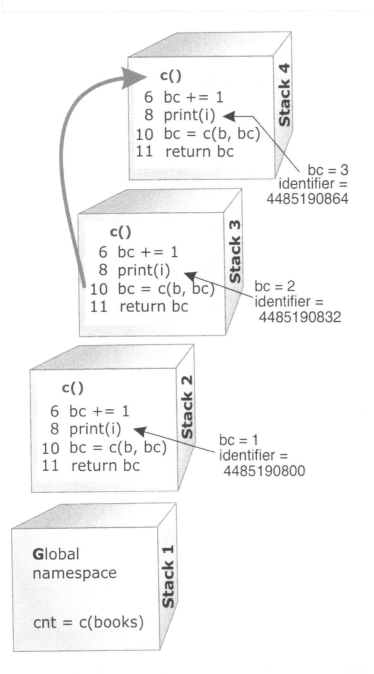

c()
6 bc += 1
8 print(i)
10 bc = c(b, bc)
11 return bc

Stack 4

bc = 3
identifier = 4485190864

c()
6 bc += 1
8 print(i)
10 bc = c(b, bc)
11 return bc

Stack 3

bc = 2
identifier = 4485190832

c()
6 bc += 1
8 print(i)
10 bc = c(b, bc)
11 return bc

Stack 2

bc = 1
identifier = 4485190800

Global namespace

Stack 1

cnt = c(books)

In **Stack 5**, the Python Interpreter runs line 11 and returns the value of "bc" to the calling function in **Stack 4**, as shown in the next diagram. In **Stack 4**, the Python Interpreter runs line 11 and returns the value of "bc" to the calling function in **Stack 3**. Next, the Python Interpreter returns "bc" to the calling function in **Stack 2**. Finally, "bc" is returned to **Stack 1** to line 16, the initial function call.

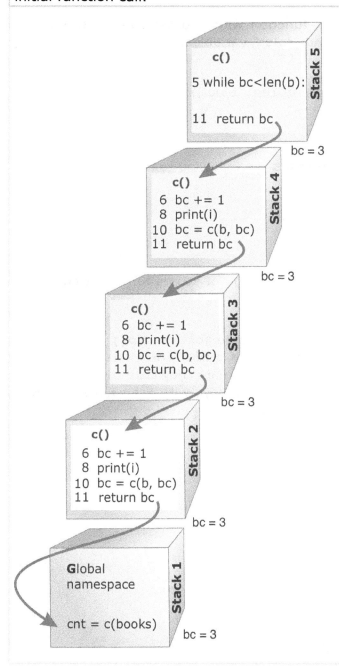

The Zip Function

Now let's look at several interesting functions. The **zip()** function takes two or more <u>iterables</u> as arguments and returns a "zip" object that behaves like tuples. For example, when you pass two lists with three elements each, zip() returns three pairs in a "zip" object.

The first example uses the **zip()** function with two lists, and returns a zip object that is <u>unpacked</u> to the "order" and "color" variables.

```
1    for order, color in zip([1, 2, 3], ['green', 'red', 'blue']):
2        print(order, color, '\n')
```

When I run the code, the Console prints the following text.

```
In [1]:
1 green
2 red
3 blue
```

In the next example, I want to create a range of scores for a plot chart with the matplotlib library.

I'm going to use 'school_Dict' as my iterable for the **zip()** function, and convert "zip" objects into a **tuple**, **dictionary**, and a **list**. The expression is a <u>list comprehension</u> that combines two zip objects to create 'newList.' The next figure shows the objects in "school_Dict." There are three keys with list values. The keys are:

> Herman
>
> John
>
> Mary

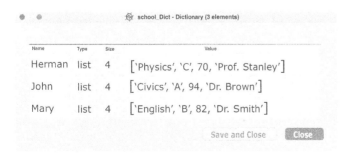

Figure 6.6   The school_Dict

In the first half of the expression I use the zip() function to combine objects together into a zip object. In the second half of the expression, I "unzip" the dictionary objects using an unpacking * operator. Now, we'll experiment in the Console and gradually work up to the final list comprehension.

```
newList = [dict(zip(school_Dict, x)) for x in zip(*school_Dict.values())]
```

1. The first half of the expression creates a zip object using "x" from the second half of the expression. As a demonstration, I'm going to temporarily provide "x" values in a tuple. In Step 4, we'll replace "x" when we use zip() to unpack the iterable from "school_Dict.values()."

    ```
    x=(('Physics', 'Civics', 'English' ),
              ('C', 'A', 'B'),
              (70, 94, 82),
              ('Prof. Stanley', 'Dr. Brown', 'Dr. Smith'))
    ```

    This "x" tuple contains the four tuples shown below. If you look back at the original **school_Dict** you can see that here I've grouped the three list items differently.

    ```
    ('Physics', 'Civics', 'English')
    ('C', 'A', 'B')
    (70, 94, 82)
    ('Prof. Stanley', 'Dr. Brown', 'Dr. Smith')
    ```

2. Let's continue looking at the first half of the list comprehension, which returns a zip object. In the **Console**, I'm going to use the tuple() function to temporarily convert this zip object to a tuple.

    ```
    In [1]:tuple(zip(school_Dict, x))

    Out[1]:
    (('Herman', ('Physics', 'Civics', 'English')),
     ('John', ('C', 'A', 'B')),
     ('Mary', (70, 94, 82)))
    ```

3. The "x" tuple in **Step 1** has the same values as the last half of the list comprehension statement.

    ```
    tuple(zip(*school_Dict.values()))
    ```

When I remove the tuple() function, this is now the same expression as the second half of the list comprehension.

zip(**school_Dict.values())

4. Now that we've looked at different zip statements, I'm going to repeat Step 1. This time I am using the **dict()** function instead of the **tuple()** function.

dict(zip(school_Dict, x))

5. Earlier, when we looked at <u>list comprehensions</u>, I said a list comprehension follows this format:

newlist = **[expression(variable) - for item in iterable- if]**

In Step 4 we created the "expression." In Step 3 we created the **iterable** statement.

expression	dict(zip(school_Dict, x))
for item in	for x in
iterable	zip(**school_Dict.values())

The two zip statements are combined into the list comprehension that follows.

newList = **[**dict(zip(school_Dict, x)) for x in zip(**school_Dict.values())**]**

Finally, to create my graph, I create a "graphNums" object using the objects in newList[2].

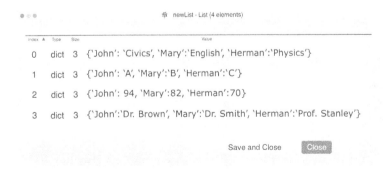

Figure 6.7 *newList*

graphNums = list(newList[2].values())

Then, I assign "graphNums" to the third element in newList[2].

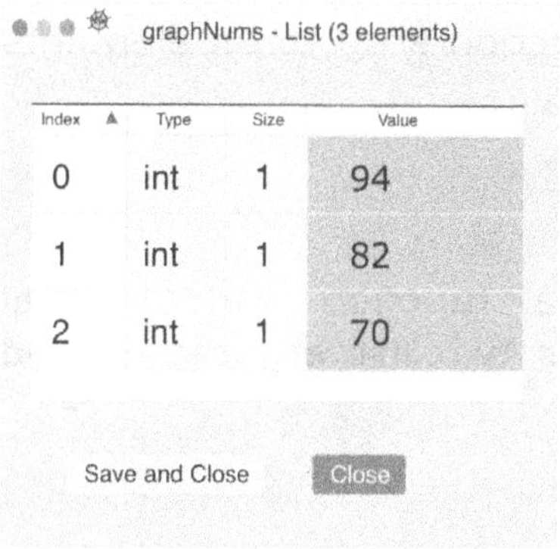

Figure 6.8   graphNums

In the next example, I create a tuple for the grades using the unpacking asterisk symbol, as shown below. The asterisk * unpacks the sequence into positional arguments and behaves like an "unzip."   The "grades" are the third element in the "s" tuple.

school_Dict = {'John': ['Civics', 'A', 94, 'Dr. Brown'],
                          'Mary': ['English', 'B', 82, 'Dr. Smith'],
                          'Herman': ['Physics', 'C', 70, 'Prof. Stanley']}

c, g, **s**, t = list(zip(*myDict.values()))

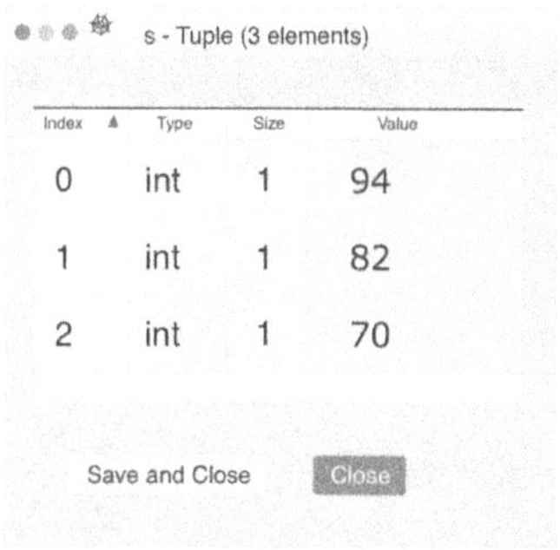

Figure 6.9   The Tuple 's'

The Map() Function

The map() function takes a unary function and a **data structure** or "iterable" as arguments and returns an iterator of type "map" that applies the function to all items in the **data structure.** Map() is a higher-order function because it acts on or returns another function.

$$map(<function>, <iterator>)$$

In this example, the map() function applies the function str() to all elements in "mylist."

$$map(str, mylist)$$

The map() function arguments can also be a function with several arguments. In the code below, the function "max" takes two list arguments and returns a "map" object.

```
1    list1, list2 = [2, 4, 6], [1, 3, 5]
2    map(max, list1, list2)
```

In the next example, I convert the "map" object type to a "list," so you can see the values returned. The max() function is applied to each list item, so the statements are 2 > 1, 4 > 3, and 6 >5.

```
In [1]: list1, list2 = [2, 4, 6], [1, 3, 5]
In [2]: list(map(max, list1, list2))
Out [2]: tuple [2, 4, 6]
```

This next example uses map to invoke the **gbp_to_usd** function for each element in the **gbp** list and return a new **usd** list.

```
1    def gbp_to_usd(temp)
2        return round(temp * .8, 2)
3
4
5    usd = []
6    gbp = [6.70, 32.51]
7    for m in map(gbp_to_usd, gbp):
8        usd.append(m)
9    print(usd)
```

The Console prints the following.

```
In [1]:
[5.36, 26.01]
```

Earlier, when we looked at <u>list comprehensions</u>, I compared them to the map() function. Lines 7 and 8 in the previous example could be rewritten as a list comprehension, as shown below on line 7.

```
1  def gbp_to_usd(temp)
2      return round(temp * .8, 2)
3
4
5  usd = []
6  gbp = [6.70, 32.51]
7  usd = [gbp_to_usd(temp) for temp in gbp]
8  print(usd)
```

Lambda Functions

<u>Lambda</u> expressions are used to create anonymous functions. These functions are not bound to a name and typically are simple expressions, often used with the map() or filter() functions. The format of a lambda expression is shown below. The <*parameters*> are variable names.

lambda *parameters*: *expression*

In the next lambda expression, on line 2 I am passing the sort() function the second element [1] in the list "pairs." The parameter is "m."

```
1  pairs = [(1, 'Jan'), (2, 'Feb'), (3, 'April')]
2  pairs.sort(key=lambda m: m[1])
```

Now the Console prints out "pairs" with the values sorted by the second element.

```
In [2]: pairs
Out[2]: [(3, 'April'), (2, 'Feb'), (1, 'Jan')]
```

In this next example, a lambda expression is combined with the map() function. The lambda parameter is "x" and the expression is **x * 4**.

```
1  for i in map(lambda x: x * 4, [1, 3, 6, 7]):
2      print(i)
```

The Console prints out the value shown below.

```
In [1]:
4
12
24
28
```

The Filter() Function

The filter() function takes a *function* and a **data structure** (*iterable*) as arguments. Filter() returns items in an iterable (of "filter" object type) for each *<iterator>* where the *<function>* returns **True** for that *<iterator>*.

filter(*<function>*, *<iterator>*)

In this example, filter() returns matched items from **myvar** as a "filter" object type, which I convert to a "list" on line 8.

```
1   def myfunc(mystr):
2       if mystr in 'Hello':
3           return True
4       else:
5           return False
6
7   myvar = ('H', 'i')
8   print(list(filter(myfunc, myvar)))
```

The Console prints out the value shown below, because "H" is in the string "Hello."

['H']

Lambda with Filter

You can also use a "lambda" expression as your function. Line 1 returns an object of type "filter" and assigns the values to "myvar." I convert the "filter" type to a "tuple" on line 2.

```
1   myvar = filter(lambda x: x > 4, [1, 3, 6, 7])
2   print(tuple(myvar))
```

The Console prints out the value shown below, because 6 and 7 are > 4.

(6, 7)

Let's look at this expression in detail. First, we'll look at the lambda function, keeping in mind the format of a lambda expression.

lambda *variable names*: *expression*

lambda expression: lambda x: x > 4	
parameter (variable names)	expression
x	x > 4

Now, let's focus on the filter part of the expression, given this format of a filter expression.

filter(*<function>*, *<iterator>*)

filter expression: filter(*<function>*, [1, 3, 6, 7]	
function	iterator
<the lambda function>	[1, 3, 6, 7]

Finally, let's put all the pieces back together.

expression: filter(lambda x: x > 4, [1, 3, 6, 7]	
function	iterator
lambda x: x > 4	[1, 3, 6, 7]

The iter() Function

The iter() function has two very different behaviors. If a second argument, *sentinel*, is given, the object must be a callable object, like a function. If the function call **iter(mylist)** includes one argument, like a list, the function iterates over the list.

iter(myfunction, *sentinel***)**

The Print() Function

Throughout this chapter, you've seen many examples of the print() function.

The print() function prints out to the Console and is a handy debugging tool.

The default behavior is to print a line return, but if you provide the "**end**" keyword argument as shown below, there is no line return. In this example, the **\n** adds a line feed before 'Hello World.'

```
print('\nHello World', end='')
```

We've seen several examples already where I changed an integer to a string before using the print() function. You can also print integers or floats. This example demonstrates how to print the result of an arithmetic expression.

```
print(2*3)
```

The console output is "6."

When we looked at recursive functions, you may have noticed the last line printed an integer and strings.

```
print('There are %d books in %s' % (cnt, books))
```

6.21 Classes

This topic provides a brief overview of classes. The **docs.python.org** website has a tutorial on classes and explains the concept of "self" in great detail.

- Create a Class
- The DocString
- Variables - Attributes
- Create an Instance of the Class
- Methods
- Dotted Notation for Attributes
- Calling a Method

When working with classes, first you define or create a "class," then you create an "instance" of the class. In the examples that follow, my class name is "Car," and my instance of "Car" is "my_car." I can reuse the class "Car," creating many instances of "Car."

Classes implement data abstractions. To work with a class, you don't need to know the details inside the class or how it gets the job done. You only need to understand the data attributes and methods of the class.

You can define a class based on another class. So, for example, I could define a class Convertible(Car). When you create a class, the superclass is in parenthesis. The class Convertible(Car) is using "Car" as the superclass. "Convertible" is the subclass of "Car."

The variable "*self*" refers to any object you create of type "Car." Continuing the earlier example, "*self*" refers to the instance "my_car." The variable "*self*" is implicitly passed as the first parameter to class attributes and methods.

Special Methods and Override Behavior

Earlier, we looked at special method names that refer to system-defined or "dunder" names that begin with two underline characters. PEP 8 covers Module Level Dunder Names. Classes inherit these special methods from parent classes but can override that behavior.

For example, in Python, you see < in comparisons, but you could override the **__lt__ (less than)** behavior to do something entirely different. "Data attributes" associated with a class definition are called "class variables." When associated with an instance of a class, they are called instance variables. Sometimes you'll see a class variable used instead of a global variable, for example to increment a counter.

A class definition begins with **def __init__(self)**, as shown below on line 4.

```
1   class Car():
2       """This class represents a car."""
3       yr = 2020
4       def __init__(self, model, make, year):
5           """Initialize model, make, and year variables."""
6           self.model = model
7           self.make = make
8           self.year = year
9       def drive(self):
10          """Move the car."""
11          print(self.model.title() + " is now moving.")
12      def parallelpark(self):
13          """Parallel park the car."""
14          print(self.model.title() + " is now parking.")
15
16
```

```
17  my_car = Car('Subaru', 'Crosstrek', 2019)
18  print(my_car.model, my_car.make, my_car.year)
19  my_car.parallelpark()
```

Create a Class

In the previous class example, line 1 creates a class named "Car." Class names begin with a capital letter to differentiate them from function names, which should be lowercase.

The DocString

Lines 2, 5, 10, and 13 look like comments but are actually examples of a "DocString."

The function help() reads the docstring when gathering information about an object.

Class Variables - Attributes

Continuing with the car class example, beginning with the function definition on line 4, you can see the four parameters in the class.

```
def __init__(self, model, make, year):
    self
    model
    make
    year
```

When working with the "my_car" instance of the Car class, I can use dotted notation to reference the variables.

my_car.model

my_car.make

my_car.year

When referring to the state of an object, you are referring to variables or **data attributes**. The variables **model**, **make**, and **year** on lines 6, 7, and 8, respectively, are accessible through instances.

```
self.model = model
self.make = make
self.year = year
```

The statement below is **invalid** because there is no attribute named "**color.**" When I run this program, the Python Interpreter raises an **AttributeError** in the **Console**.

my_car.color

Instance Variables and Class Variables

Instance variables are unique to each instance of the class. For example, **my_car.model** is different than **my_car2.model**. However, all instances of a class share class variables and methods. All instances of the **Car** class share the class variable "**yr**" I created on line 3.

Create an Instance of the Class

Instantiation is when you create an instance of an object from a class. On line 17, I create an instance of the Car class named "**my_car.**"

my_car = Car('Subaru', 'Crosstrek', 2019)

Instance objects have attribute references. Valid attribute names include "**data attributes**" and "**methods.**"

Methods

Functions that are part of a class are referred to as a "**methods**" or "**method attributes.**" When referring to the behavior of an object, you are discussing the function or method. The "Car" class has two methods, defined in lines 9 and 12. The "drive" method is shown below.

```
def drive(self):
    """Move the car."""
    print(self.model.title() + " is now moving.")
```

Dotted Notation for Attributes

The normal dotted notation "**object.variable**" is used to access the instance of the class (the object) and the attribute. In this example, the syntax is "**my_car.model.**" The primary object instance is "**my_car,**" and the attribute identifier name is "**model.**" To refer to the model, make, or year attributes, follow the syntax on line 18, as shown below.

print(my_car.model, my_car.make, my_car.year)

Calling a Method

To call a method in a class instance, use the syntax shown in line 19.

```
my_car.parallelpark()
```

These two statements call a method. The statement syntax varies, but the statements do the same thing.

```
Car.drive(my_car)
my_car.drive()
```

Superclass and Subclass

In this example the subclass "Family(Person)" is reusing the Person.__ init__(self, name). This makes the superclass attributes "name" and "alive" available to the class "Family."

```
class Person(object):
    def __init__(self, name):
            self.name = name
            self.alive = True

class Family(Person):
    def __init__(self, name, relationshiop):
            Person.__init__(self, name)
            self.relationship = relationship
```

At the end of this book, the **Appendix - Reference** has links for more information on Classes, Functions, Methods, Attributes, and Instances.

6.22 Modules and Libraries

Variables in Imported Modules

Often modules are broken into separate files or libraries, and you add these to your code with the **import** statement. This idea of breaking code into smaller chunks of code that are easy to debug and reuse independently is known as

modularity. Typically you don't need to know anything about the internal code in a function or module. All you really care about is the function inputs (arguments), what the function does, and what the function outputs (the return object.) This concept is known as **abstraction**.

To reference a variable inside another module, use dotted notation. In this example, I import a module "mymodule2" that has the variable "mystr2." The expression **mymodule2.mystr2** returns the value of **mystr2**.

```
import mymodule2

print(mymodule2.mystr2)
```

To avoid name conflicts, you can also provide a function "alias" with your import statement. The syntax to assign an alias "plot" is shown below.

```
import matplotlib pyplot as plot
```

6.23 Attributes

The Python glossary entry for "attributes" is "a value associated with an object which is referenced by name using dotted expressions."

```
myint = 57
print(myint.upper)
```

When this program runs, it causes an unhandled exception, and the **Console** Traceback message is "**AttributeError**," because there is no attribute "upper" for a variable of type "int."

When looking at Classes in this chapter, we saw that attributes could be variables or methods within a class instance. In our earlier Class example, we saw that instance objects have attribute references. Valid attribute names include "**data attributes**" and "**methods**." In the example below of attributes, "**yr**" is a class variable, and "**drive**" is a method in the **my_car** instance of the "**Car**" Class.

```
my_car.yr

my_car.drive()
```

6.24 Scope, Namespace & Memory

Each time a program runs and creates variables, the Python Interpreter adds the variables to the "global namespace" or "**Stack 1**." This top-level code executes at the '**__main__**' scope, as outlined at docs.python.org. The *global namespace* is the first memory "stack."

Variable Explorer displays objects in the current "scope." Variable Explorer is empty until you run the program to create the program's memory "namespace."

The variable "name" combined with the memory "space" (or namespace) uniquely identifies a variable. When you step through your code, the "local scope" or local namespace reflects the objects in memory at that point in time. Scope changes when your code moves into a method or function, and a new "local scope" is created while you're inside that function. Lexical scoping or "static scoping" refers to the line of code that created a variable and limits the variable to that local scope or namespace.

The LEGB rule refers to the **L**ocal -> **E**nclosing -> **G**lobal -> **B**uilt-in namespaces. Nested functions consist of a "local" namespace located within the "enclosing" function. All functions are stacked onto the "global" namespace, which in turn is stacked on top of Python's built-in namespace. We'll look at several examples of local and global scope at the end of this chapter.

In Python, you can read, but not change, the value of a global variable at any point in your program and from within functions, as long as everything is within the **same *.py file**. It is possible to have two variables with the same name and different values because they are in two different "scopes." You'll notice this behavior as you step through the code and watch the list of variables in Variable Explorer. When you step into a function, the variable names reflect the "local scope."

If you want to change a variable in different "scopes," you can use the "**global**" keyword to change the variable into a "global variable" so that you can change the variable within that paritcular local scope. We looked at global variables earlier with an example of how object values change as "scope" changes.

There are several functions to view scope, and we'll look at a few in the following pages. For example, the keyword "**nonlocal**" refers to a variable in the "enclosing" namespace. As you work with these functions, you'll see that namespaces in Python are stored in the form of a dictionary.

dir(__builtins__)

locals()

<u>globals()</u>

<u>id()</u>

We looked at memory stacks for <u>recursive functions</u> earlier.

A Function that Accesses a Global Variable

We'll begin looking at namespaces and scope in the example below. The function definition for **blockParty()** begins on line 1, and the function has no arguments. The indented lines that follow through line 3 make up the body of the **blockParty()** function. Lines 1 to 3 are a "suite of code." The main body of the program begins on line 6.

- The "food" variable is defined on line 6 in the main body of the program, which means "food" is in the *global namespace*. Any function in this *.py file can access the global "food." In this example, within the **blockParty()** function, the global variable "food" is accessed on line 3.

- The **blockParty()** function is **not allowed to change** the value in the global "food" variable.

```
1   def blockParty()
2       name = 'John'
3       print(name, 'has', food)
4
5
6   food = 'chips'
7   blockParty()
```

Variables in the main program are in the *Global Namespace* of the program. The main program begins on line 6. In the diagram that follows this is memory "Stack 1." In order to see the scope changing "live" in Variable Explorer, we're going to debug the file.

1. Type the sample code into the **Editor**. If it's not already open, open Variable Explorer from the **View** menu by clicking on **Panes**. At this point,

there are no variables displayed because we haven't run the program to initialize the variables and assign values. That's about to change!

On the Spyder toolbar, click on **Debug file** (Ctrl+F5).

2. In the **Editor** pane, line 1 is highlighted. Because line 1 is a function definition, when I click **Run current line** (Ctrl+F10), the Python Interpreter analyzes the function definition and then moves to line 6.

    In the **iPython Console**, to the left of line 6 is an arrow ----> indicating the Python Interpreter is about to run line 6.

    In the Spyder toolbar, click **Run current line**. Line 6 runs. Now, in the **Editor** pane, the cursor moves down and highlights line 7. In the iPython Console, the arrow ----> now points to line 7.

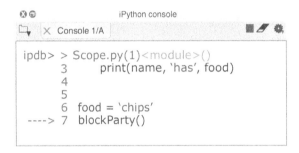

    Variable Explorer displays the variable "food" with a value of "chips." Notice the variable is a "str" type.

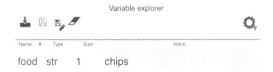

3. Line 7 invokes the function **blockParty()**. We want to step through the code inside the function. In the Spyder toolbar, click on Step into function or method of current line (Ctrl+F11). Line 7 runs invoking the **blockParty()** function.

    If you click **Run current line** *instead of "Step into function or method of current line," the program runs all lines in the* **blockParty()** *function and exits debug mode.*

    In the iPython Console, debug moves the cursor to the function **blockParty()** on line 1. An arrow ----> points to line 1.

The Editor highlights line 1.

```
1  def blockParty()
2      name = 'John'
3      print(name, 'has', food)
4
5
6  food = 'chips'
7  blockParty()
```

In the Spyder toolbar, click **Run current line** to run line 1. The local scope changes to the **blockParty()** function and a new "stack" of memory is created. In the next diagram, this is "**Stack 2**." Variable Explorer still shows the "food" variable because "food" is in the *global namespace*. The global scope variables can be accessed or "read," **but not changed**, within the **blockParty()** function.

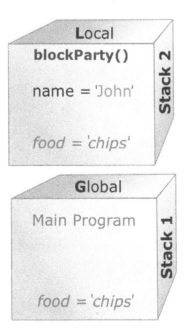

4.   The previous diagram outlines the *global namespace* in **Stack 1**, and the *local namespace* of the function **blockParty()** in **Stack 2**.

In the **iPython Console**, let's look at the *global namespace* with the built-in function **globals()**. Below, I've abbreviated the output text to show the last line, which is my global variable "food." The interpreter actually prints out a large dictionary for the namespace, as indicated by the curly braces **{}**.

ipdb> globals()

{ .... 'food': 'chips'}

5.   Continue stepping through the code. In the function **blockParty()** after line 2 runs, Variable Explorer also shows the "name" variable. This variable is in **Stack 2** or the *local namespace*.

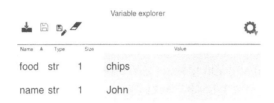

When you run line 3, the iPython Console output is "John has chips."

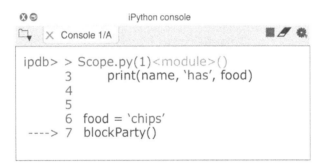

6.   The locals() function shows all variables in the current or *local namespace* **Stack 2**. In the iPython Console, type "locals()." Because "food" is in the global namespace, it is not shown.

ipdb> locals()

{'name': 'John'}

7.   Continue stepping through the code. In the function **blockParty()**, after line 3 runs, the Python Interpreter moves down to line 7. When line 7 is highlighted, you are back in the main program or *global namespace*. The *global namespace*, or **Stack 1**, has the "food" variable with a value of 'chips.'

Variable Explorer no longer shows the "name" variable because **Stack 2** is discarded when you exit the **blockParty()** function.

A Function Variable with the Same Name as a Global Variable

The previous example is pretty straightforward. Now we are going to repeat the same steps with a small variation. This time we add a "food" variable assignment on line 3 within the function "**blockParty()**."

As we step through the code, you'll see two variables named "food," but with different values and identifiers.

```
1   def blockParty()
2       name = 'John'
3       food = 'salsa'
4       print(name, 'has', food)
5
6
7   food = 'chips'
8   blockParty()
```

The main program begins on line 7. The "food" variable from line 7 is in the *Global Namespace* or main scope of the program. The diagram in Step 4 that follows shows this as memory "**Stack 1**."

Now we'll debug the file.

1. Type the sample code into the **Editor**. On the Spyder toolbar, click on **Debug file** (Ctrl+F5).

    If it's not already open, open Variable Explorer from the **View** menu by clicking on **Panes**.

2. In the **Editor** pane, line 1 is highlighted. Because line 1 is a function definition, when you click **Run current line** (Ctrl+F10) the Python Interpreter evaluates the function definition and moves on to line 7.

    In the **iPython Console**, to the left of line 7 is an arrow ----> indicating the Python Interpreter is about to run line 7.

    In the Spyder toolbar, click **Run current line**. Line 7 runs. The program is still in the "*global namespace*" or "**Stack 1**."

    In the Editor pane, debug moves down and highlights line 8. The iPython Console displays an arrow next to line 8, as shown in the next diagram.

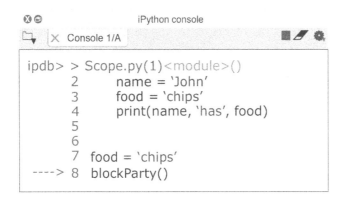

3. Line 8 invokes the function **blockParty()**. We want to step through the code inside the function. In the Spyder toolbar, click on Step into function or method of current line (Ctrl+F11). Line 8 runs invoking the **blockParty()** function.

    In the **iPython Console**, debug moves the cursor to the function **blockParty()** on line 1. In the Console, an arrow ----> points to line 1. In the Editor, line 1 is also highlighted. In the Spyder toolbar, click **Run current line** to run line 1.

    The local scope changes to the **blockParty()** function, and a new "stack" of memory is created. This is "**Stack 2**" and is now the "local scope." Variable Explorer still shows the "food" variable with a value of "chips" from the *global namespace*.

4. Continue stepping through the code. In the function **blockParty()**, after line 2 runs, Variable Explorer shows the "name" and "food" variables. The "food" variable is from the *global namespace*.

    Stack 2 now has two variables: the local variable "name" and the global variable "food."

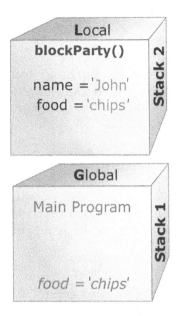

5. When you run line 3, a new variable called "food" is created in "**Stack 2**" with a different value of "salsa," as shown below in Variable Explorer.

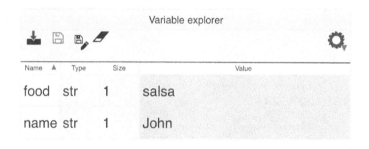

    This local variable "food" in **Stack 2** has the same name as the global variable but points to a different location in memory - in this case, **Stack 2**'s "food" with the value "salsa."

6. This time, the locals() function shows two variables in the current or *local namespace*, which is **Stack 2**. In the iPython Console, type "locals()."

    ipdb> locals()

    {'name': 'John', 'food': 'salsa'}

    Looking at the printout in the **iPython Console**, you can tell the namespace variables are stored in a dictionary because of the **curly braces {}**. The program is within the **Stack 2** *local namespace* of

blockParty(). If I were to update the local variable "food," the other "food" variable in the outer scope or *global namespace* would not change.

To see the identifier of the objects, let's use the **id()** function to get the ID for the **Stack 2** "food" variable. Because line 4 is highlighted in the Editor, I know I am still in the *local namespace* of the blockParty() function. Your computer output for ID will be different than what is shown below.

> **ipdb**> id(food)
>
> 140309822725104

7. Continue stepping through the code. After line 4 runs, the code moves down to line 7. When line 7 is highlighted, you are back in the *global namespace* or **Stack 1**.

   Variable Explorer no longer shows the "name" variable because *Stack 2 is discarded* when you exit the "blockParty()" function. Also, you'll notice the value of the "food" variable changed back to "chips." The program is back in the *global namespace* or "Stack 1.

8. In the iPython Console, use the id() function to view the identifier for this "food" variable in the *global namespace*. This output will show a different ID number.

   > ipdb> id(food)
   >
   > 140309822723824

Scope in Nested Functions

Earlier we looked at the LEGB rule for **L**ocal -> **E**nclosing -> **G**lobal -> **B**uilt-in namespaces. Nested functions consist of a function's "local" namespace located within the "enclosing" function. To illustrate the "enclosing namespace," the next example has a nested function, "**games()**."

```
1   def blockParty()
2       def games()
3           game = 'darts'
4           print(game, 'starts at noon')
5       name = 'John'
6       food = 'salsa'
7       print(name, 'has', food)
8
```

```
 9
10  food = 'chips'
11  blockParty()
```

The scope of the function **blockParty()** is the "enclosing namespace" of the **games()** function, and is **Stack 2**. The function **games()** is nested inside **blockParty()** and will be **Stack 3**.

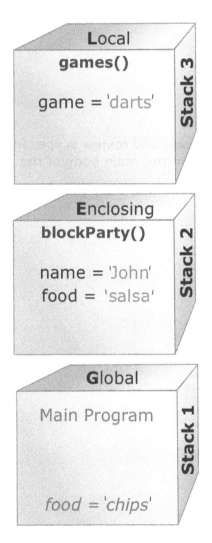

Earlier I said the "global" keyword is used when you want to update a global variable from within a function. Similarly, the nested function **games()** can update "name" in **blockparty()'s** "enclosing" namespace if you add a statement on line 3 with the keyword "nonlocal."

```
1   def blockParty()
2       def games()
3           nonlocal name
4           game = 'darts'
5           print(game, 'starts at noon')
6       name = 'John'
7       food = 'salsa'
8       print(name, 'has', food)
9       games()
10
11
12  food = 'chips'
13  blockParty()
```

Let's add another function to the code and review scope. In this example, the **events()** function definition is on line 11 in the main body of the program.

```
1   def blockParty()
2       def games()
3           game = 'darts'
4           print(game, 'starts at noon')
5       name = 'John'
6       food = 'salsa'
7       print(name, 'has', food)
8       games()
9
10
11  def events()
12      type = 'party'
13      print(type)
14
15  food = 'chips'
16  blockParty()
18  events()
```

In this case, the main program has two paths. The functions blockParty() and games() have no access to the variables in the events() function, and vice versa.

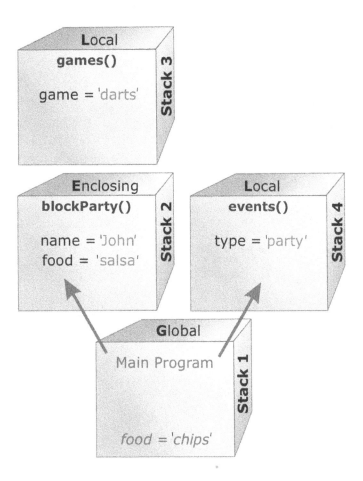

When you're analyzing scopes, *diagram the path* through the program to determine namespaces.

7. Conclusion

Einstein said, "If you can't explain it simply, you don't understand it well enough." Learning new things is a passion of mine, and I've found the process of organizing notes, creating illustrations, and pondering how to craft clear examples helps me grasp concepts. Then too, it's nice to go back in a year when I've forgotten something and refer to a solid example.

Thank you for reading along with me through the interesting topics and less than thrilling subjects. If the result is you have mastered new features, it was worth it! I'd love to hear the cool things you're doing with Python, so please don't hesitate to leave comments in a review.

Index

www.ingramcontent.com/pod-product-compliance
Lightning Source LLC
Chambersburg PA
CBHW060600060326
40690CB00017B/3777